*HOW
TO GIVE
YOUR
CHILDREN
EVERYTHING
THEY
REALLY
NEED*

How
to give
your
children
everything
they
really
need

EDMUND W. JANSS

Tyndale House
Publishers, Inc.
Wheaton, Illinois

ACKNOWLEDGMENTS

Warm appreciation is
expressed for these dear
friends for help in making
this book possible:
Dr. Stanley Mooneyham
Dr. Ted Engstrom
Mr. Paul Van Oss

for their continued
encouragement:
Peter Lee
Fram Jehangir
Bhaskar Sojwal
Maureen Lampard

for help in gathering case
history background:
Terri Owens

for persevering help and
editing in the preparation
of these pages:
Olive, my wife

for patience during the
pacings, contemplations,
and absentmindedness
during the gestation:
*my children and
grandchildren,*
who have always been
reluctant but kindly subject
as I prepared my book
and articles on child care.

Library of Congress
Catalog Card
Number 79-63461.
ISBN 0-8423-1520-9,
paper. Copyright © 1979
by Edmund W. Janss.

Second printing, October
1979. Printed in the United
States of America.

CONTENTS

FOREWORD

Let me tell you how the whole focus of my life was changed through one little girl. I am doing the work I do today because of Jung Hi in Korea.

It was over twenty years ago, but I still remember her case-history and picture that I received from Christians in that country. Her tiny face was so sad. Her clothes were ragged. Her story was simple: "Found on the streets of Pusan. Parents dead. Taken to a Christian orphanage."

I wrote to her, received little notes in return, and found beautiful new dimension coming into my life. She became a part of our family, even though thousands of miles stretched between us, and we supported her for over ten years until she was grown.

One wonderful day I even met her out in Korea. We spent a memorable day together, walking the orphanage grounds with her shy little hand in mine. Such "parenthood" does something for one, even when it may only be long-distance foster parenthood. And it did something for her too. I'll never forget that simple-but-precious note which came weeks after my visit: "Every day since you were here, 'dear father,' I remember the touch of your real hand, and the sound of your real voice."

The story of parenthood is the pivot of history. On it hinge the Bible and the human heart. And it is the story told by my good friend, Ed Janss, found in the following pages about the living relationship between two souls—parent and child.

Larry Ward, President
Food for the Hungry
Scottsdale, Arizona

INTRODUCTION

In December of 1960 on a return trip from the Orient, I stopped in Hawaii to catch my breath after jet lag. While there I visited a Methodist church in Honolulu and heard the pastor speak on the subject, "The Forgotten Man of Christmas." I do not recall the young minister's name, but I do remember the sermon. The "forgotten man" turned out to be Joseph, the husband of Mary.

The sermon dealt with the kind of man Joseph was and the type of home that he and Mary created as the earthly influence on the growing Lord. (He "increased in wisdom and stature, and in favour with God and man.")

"Where," he asked, "did Jesus (at the earthly level) learn that God was loving like a father? True, he was led of the Spirit, but he was also a real human child and undoubtedly saw a model, though admittedly an imperfect one, in Joseph.

"Where did he learn we should be a neighbor to all? Possibly by watching Joseph and Mary perform deeds of kindness along the streets of Nazareth.

"Where did he learn that a heavenly Father is accepting of all, no matter what the misdeed? Perhaps by seeing Joseph and Mary open their hearts to Jesus' erring brothers and sisters.

"Where did he learn about poise and self-respect? Possibly by watching Joseph walk the streets of the village with dignity and a sense of worth. He could later take Leviticus

19:18 ("Thou shalt love thy neighbour as thyself") and impregnate it with meaning for friends as well as for self-identity.

"When did Jesus first learn that forgiveness was available to all, both high and low, rich and poor, Jew and Gentile? Perhaps by observing a mother and father opening their hearts to all. Later he was to show equal remission for Mary Magdalene and Zaccheus.

"How did he know that God expected the very best from his children? By the patience of Joseph in the carpentry shop in the creation of craftsmanlike furniture?"

The pastor drew other inferences from Gospel passages regarding the nature of that little home overlooking the Nazarene valley. He deduced the image of the parent and the home as the concept the Child carried through his life. The young Man's *earthly* ideas of God, society, and universe were imprinted from early impressions as he observed parental love in the way they reacted to others and the world. Child psychologist Fritz Kunkel comments that during tender babyhood the parent "is" God. Later revelation taught Jesus his peculiar sonship as the Spirit increasingly confirmed to the growing Lord truths at an eternal level, all part of the mystery of the incarnation. But I am convinced that the preincarnate Lord was planning and preparing such a home as this for himself before the foundation of the world.

For the past two decades I have worked for two major Christian agencies that specialize in child care—Christian Children's Fund of Virginia and World Vision International of California. The major leaders of these two groups, Dr. J. Calvitt Clarke and Dr. W. Stanley Mooneyham, although from different economic backgrounds, had surprisingly similar familial settings as children. Growing up within these home environments (which reflected in many ways the Nazareth home), they developed a driving love for helpless children.

In 1961 I wrote a book concerning the effects of Calvitt Clarke's childhood on his vocation in child care. In reviewing my book, the *Los Angeles Times* said, "J. Calvitt Clarke seeks for these children a warm family atmosphere."

More recently, I have been studying the boyhood of Stan Mooneyham and its likely effects on his warm-hearted response to starving youngsters. Commenting in 1973 on some 123 such waifs he saw in Cambodia, he reflected this deep domestic concern:

"Today I visited one of the forts that surrounds the besieged city of Phnom Penh. Here I saw the largest group of war orphans I have seen together—123 of them; all boys—living together. They are only a fraction of the total, for there are an estimated 17,000 orphans—the waifs of war—in the country.

"Standing on top of the dirt which formed one side of the triangular-shaped fort, I was reminded of my early Boy Scout camps. Small fires dotted the camp site; on each one was a canteen cup filled with boiling water, cooking the hardness out of a tiny handful of green beans. This was their lunch. One boy was cutting up a small fish which would add a little protein to the thin soup.

"It took the sight of guns to remind me that this was no game —no scout jamboree. It was deadly business, and the boys knew it better than I did. What anguish was hidden behind those stoic little faces I could never know.

"The oldest boy was fourteen. The youngest five. I stopped to talk with the oldest, and with my Khmer colleague interpreting, he readily answered my questions.

"Mother and father? Doesn't know where they are. They disappeared during a battle in his village. He ran and ran. He thinks they are dead. His brothers and sisters may be in Phnom Penh. But he doesn't know where to start looking for them among hundreds of thousands of refugees.

"What does he do now? Works with the other boys; they train to protect themselves. Can he shoot a gun? He shakes his head in a vigorous yes.

"Who cooks his food? He does—as do all the other boys. Pointing to his canteen cup, I ask if this is all he has to eat. Again he nods yes. I am told that rice is too expensive and there is no money.

"I pull out some money from my pocket and hand them [sic] to the lieutenant who informally runs the camp. I ask him to buy some rice for the boys. The interpreter tells the boys, and they smile broadly. I tell them that I hope we can do more later.

"I look into their faces. They are my little ones, too, I thought. They and all the lonely and anguished children of the world. They are my little ones—and the Lord's."

In discussing this incident with Stan after he returned, I asked him for his underlying motivation in loving children. He opened his Testament to Luke and read about that moment when "Jesus stood a little child beside him and said to the disciples, 'Anyone who takes care of a little child like this *is caring for me*! And whoever is caring for me is *caring for God* who sent me. Your care for others is the measure of your greatness.' "

Stan Mooneyham was born in 1926 into a sharecropper's family in Mississippi. Underfed children were something he knew about from babyhood. He beheld sights of hunger on all sides. Several times he himself felt the pangs during the hard winter of 1932 when farmers were being squeezed out of their precarious business.

One thing he learned at that time, however, was the value of a loving father and mother. He remembers waiting anxiously each twilight as his dad returned from the fields, bone-weary. Scott Mooneyham never tired of taking young Stan on his lap and rocking restfully as he hummed some favorite hymn.

In the late twenties and early thirties, Stan witnessed the breakup of many homes, as fathers wandered away in search of food for the family—never to return. Sometimes his young mind worried as he looked out at the scraggly cotton plants and corn stalks and waited for his own father. Always he sighed with relief when his dad trudged into sight. It was an experience that would form a basic Christian philosophy. Later it would mold his theory of child care for World Vision (of which he would become president thirty years hence).

Family support through the years became for Stan foundational to his faith. His mother was for years a local evangelist. Around the fireplace each evening as they opened the Bible, Adeline would limn out those things she felt were underlying truths of life—matters fundamental to her preaching and living ministry. In later years Stan would remember her message on the prodigal and the love of the

father. It became in his adulthood basic doctrine to his own
pulpit preaching.

When he joined the Navy in 1942 Stan would follow prodigal
paths himself for a brief while. But his mother's words
and his father's love haunted him. In Augustine's words, his
mother's dedication followed him: "It was her earnest care that
Thou my God should be my father."

The image of the perfect Father had been planted in Stan's
mind early. As he and his six brothers and sisters learned Bible
verses at family devotion times, they were often those related
to this theme: "Your heavenly Father knows that you need
these things." Other passages like it reinforced the concept.
Parents take God's place on earth to care for children—this
became the model of Stan's universe. God meant that his
world should be like a family, and the gospel invited all into a
redeeming relationship with him.

Later as Stan and his wife, LaVerda, formed their own family,
their children were to see this replica of the heavenly household
modeling. In 1969 as he took the helm of World Vision, the
same concept of family-patterning was to become fundamental
in his caring for 30,000 needy children. In ten years he would
see that figure increase five-fold to 150,000 needy youngsters
in forty-eight countries.

As Stan had grown he had learned much about the pain of
cold and hunger. Many of his playmates had been black as well
as white, although, early on, he had not known any difference.
His neighborhood of slash-pine and cotton was openly rural
and each person had depended on his neighbor while a stricken
nation struggled with 20,000,000 unemployed and a spiraling
scarcity. He recalls accompanying his mother one day as
she took a basket of turnips and potatoes to a famished family.
The wide eyes of hungry tots peering out the window and
the wonder in them as they gazed at the hoe cakes and
vegetables reinforced his own experience. Coupled with the
ache that his own small stomach had felt the previous winter,
he suddenly became aware of a universal human condition—
starvation. This haunting vision was to be articulated
in 1976 in his book, *What Do You Say to a Hungry World?*

That evening after the food-distribution to the neighbors, he reminisces, his mother sat at the foot of his bed and read him the story of the kindly Samaritan. "And," he recalls, "I never remember my mother turning anyone from our door. Whenever she heard of someone hungry, sick, or dying, she shared out of our meager supply."

Thus through the years, a clear vision of the Nazareth home and its implications for himself and the world became coupled with his experience of the Lord and of life. God was preparing him for a special role to demonstrate the love of God in practical terms.

These pages will attempt to show how this dimension of love, God's and man's, can change the lives of children, our own and the world's.

ONE
LOVING YOUR CHILD

"Love your child!" Every parent on six continents has heard it.

But how do we know when we are *loving* the child and not *using* him? That is a harder question. There is often a thin line between love and neurotic need, and it is easy to mislabel. Our emotions frequently deceive us.

Last year in Asia I went to a picnic with some of our boarding school children. They looked so neat in their blue skirts or trousers. As they sat on the green grass and ate their lunch, I noticed a five-year-old girl peering shyly around a tree. She had a lovely little face with large brown eyes, but no hands, only stumps. She was terribly thin, and around her neck hung a bag that she used to collect alms.

One of the teachers gave some food to an older boy and pointed to the little girl. He finally persuaded the youngster to come closer, and at last she sat on the grass with the others, enjoying the picnic. As the day wore on, the children began to beg the headmistress to take her home with them. The little one looked so eager and helpless that they finally prevailed, and she was made a member of the "family." My heart was gladdened as one more child came into our World Vision care.

But the joy was short-lived. That evening the child's mother came for her, and she left, weeping. Her mother said she was needed for begging—a common occurrence in the Far East.

Probably within her own definition of "love," that mother felt she was measuring up. In her mind, the corporate need of the family took precedence over the needs of the child. In her way, she "loved" the child. Perhaps as a child, the mother herself had received similar treatment and considered it the norm. Probably in her desperation, she could not even speculate on the word "love."

In 1957 I conducted a survey of a Parent-Teacher's Association on the north shore of Long Island. Among questions I included in the questionnaire were:

What do you mean by the term "parental love"?

Do you think it important that a child *feel* loved?

Please list some of the negative things you believe parents do to show "love."

Is it enough to touch and fondle the child in order to demonstrate love?

Is it necessary to sacrifice for the child to show love?

Will much protection demonstrate parental love for the child?

Does spending a lot of time with him show parental love to the child?

Will giving many nice gifts convince a child of parental love?

Does lots of praise indicate love to the child?

Will being proud of the child and expressing it often illustrate love?

The answers from several hundred parents showed an interesting variety:

50 percent felt that fondling and touching the child were vital —if coupled with other types of care. Studies at Case Western University recently indicate the validity of this view. The mother that cuddles her baby immediately after birth is, interestingly, less likely to become divorced later in life. The child responds to others better as he grows. And the mother herself tends to kiss and caress the child in later stages; this is a process known as "bonding."

37 percent expressed a need for sacrificing for the child
—although not to the extent of martyrdom.

66 percent felt that protection was vital—but not over-
protection.

25 percent felt that spending much time with the child was
important. (This community was an upper middle class one,
where parents were very busy with extra-domestic duties in the
community or business. Many fathers were traveling
constantly, and time was at a premium.)

77 percent expressed a need to give "nice gifts" to their
children as an expression of parental love (again an evidence
of that affluent New York society attempting to demonstrate
love with "things").

80 percent said that constant praise was essential to make the
child feel important and loved.

78 percent, not surprisingly, said that feeling pride for the
child was a corollary to praise. "After all," jotted one, "unless
I feel proud of my child, how can he feel pride in himself?"

"Parents, love your children," says Scripture. And as
Christians we have heard it all our lives. We know that children
"need love." We have all read how the child deprived of it
can wither and die. "Love your child," as we have said above,
has become an international cliché.

With all of this good advice, it is sad to realize that many
children *do not feel loved*. In our Korean baby homes the
nurses carry abandoned babies on their backs. This warmth at
an early age is vital to their survival. But physical contact must
be accompanied by other things. Ruffling the hair or hugging
alone is not sufficient to convince the child he is loved. Valuing
the child will demonstrate this.

Martyrdom for the child is not love. We had one housemother, now gone to glory, who gave eighteen hours a day,
seven days a week, in an orphanage. She wore herself into an
early grave. But she did it daily with a grumble and a sigh.
She was not loved nor, sadly, did she love.

Another housemother in a neighboring home gave half that
time but was a joy. Her face glowed as she enjoyed each

child in her cottage. They *felt* loved and loved her in return.

1. The survey indicated that 75 percent *rejected over-protection* as a definition of love. Through discussion they stated parents should not "hover over a child." If a child is not allowed to slowly assume autonomy he begins to feel incompetent since oversolicitousness saps the child's self-respect.

2. Another insight at the same PTA was that it is *not the amount of time* spent with a child but the *quality of time* that is important. It is said of Susannah Wesley that although she had nineteen children, she spent one hour a week alone with each. The *quality of the time* spent must have been superb, for we see what resulted in John and Charles Wesley.

3. *The parent who spends much time, but with negation* and criticism, detracts from the child's self-respect:

"Stand up straight!"
"Don't shuffle."
"You always do it wrong."

These denials can fill an hour and prove that time alone is not the sum total of love.

4. And (need I say it to Christians?) *lavishing possessions on a child is not loving him.* I know of a parent who is so busy that he cannot give attention to his child. Hence he tries to substitute *things*. Our workers have devised a short checklist as a test for each gift:

Am I giving my child this surprise because I never had one as a child?
Am I giving it because doing so agrees with my concept of a "good" parent?
Am I giving it because it is easier than communicating with her?

5. "My son is the best player on the team." *Such emphasis or exaggeration of the child's ability is not love.* Most children are predictably average. An untrue picture of his achievements can make a child feel inadequate. It creates a gap so that he cannot feel loved for his *real* self.

6. *Putting a child in a position in which a parent must always feel proud of him* adds to his anxiety. The youngster feels such love depends on achievement.

One of our former homes in Korea overspecialized in musical training. Every child was required to play an instrument honorifically. Result: most of the children graduated playing with some skill and brought great honor to the home. But few of the children felt loved!

Thus far we have seen some of the *things that parental love is not*. But in the light of Jesus' boyhood home, what are some of the elements that constitute true parental love?

TRUE PARENTAL LOVE

As we study our Lord's life we become aware of his ability for genuine dialogue and encounter. At the human level he learned this as a boy in Galilee. Luke particularly points up Jesus' acuity in communication with little children. He could focus his loving attention in a way that we mortals cannot. But we can learn much from studying his methods:

1. *The child was aware of Jesus' real love.* Each youngster he met knew he or she had Jesus' affection. The disciples tried to turn them away. Jesus took them on his lap and talked warmly to them.

Not long ago I saw the two attitudes clearly illustrated. One housemother in Thailand was pushing a crying child away from her skirt as she gossiped with a neighbor. Another worker later that same day was taking a quiet walk with a little girl holding her hand. There was a soft warmth on the worker's face. And the sparkle in the child's eyes was evidence enough that genuine encounter was in progress. The attention of the mother was focused and real.

2. *A child is also aware when love is not there.* Sometimes this is due to a thoughtless diversion. Recently my granddaughter Erin begged me to tell her a story about her toy bear "Theal." I started out well, I believe. But as the story moved along, my mind wandered and I inserted nonsensical phrases. My mind was on plans for that evening, but Erin was quickly aware that a gap between her and me was growing. This is known as distancing. She became restless, climbed down from my lap and started playing with her dolls. I had "left" her so she left me. In the I-thou encounter between two persons,

there must be an inner presence of both parties.

Let me give a paraphrase to a well-known verse—"With their lips they communicate with me, but their hearts are far from me." Rollo May has called this attitude "alienation." Estrangement, playing it cool, withdrawal of feeling, indifference, ennui, depersonalization—they all indicate a distance between two souls.

Such apartness can make a child feel unloved. It was distancing that sent the prodigal back to his father, where he found warmth and acceptance.

3. *Lack of encounter causes the gap.* How often a mother will hear a child chatting beside her and yet be preoccupied. The inattentive "yes, dear," or "that's lovely, son," while the child pours out a victory or defeat, can smother love. If a parent does this frequently enough, the child registers not love but indifference. This too creates a distance between parent and child.

Although many people believe the opposite of love is hate, it is really indifference. This is what broke the heart of God in Revelation: "You are neither hot nor cold; I wish you were one or the other! But since you are lukewarm I will spew you out of my mouth."

4. *Being at a distance causes your child to feel unloved.* But personal encounter with your child makes him feel loved. He or she subconsciously says, "I must be important. My mother takes time to get through to me!"

One of the boys who eventually became president of a Central American country came from one of our homes. He was from a poor background and his father had died when he was little. Taken into the residential part of the school, he recalls the turning point in his life. "Pastor Beckdahl took a personal interest in me. His wife mothered and guided me. Their genuine interest led me through the years. They were never too busy."

5. *Activism negates true encounter.* The "overly busy" house-parent cannot devote proper attention to the child.

The sad case of Sato shows us what can happen. He was one

of the promising boys in the Shinko-do-men Home in Japan in the 1960s. His housefather was very demanding of all the boys in the institution—but particularly of Sato. The housefather decided he would be the shining example for the home, but he was also very busy. With prosperity in Japan came rising prices and stricter demands by the government, until the houseparent did "not have time" for Sato. The boy floundered in his studies and eventually failed his college entrance exam. The pressure was too much and his "father" was too busy hurrying from one task to another. He had little time for his boys. One night in an act of final desperation, Sato hung himself from the frame of his closet door. In being busy for Sato's physical good, the housefather had neglected Sato.

A parent needs to ask himself about priorities: "Do schedules, possessions, or my children come first?" One contemporary theologian has said, "The meaning of life is in meeting." The child-parent encounter should be a genuine meeting of hearts as in the parable. "The father saw him coming and was filled with love and ran and embraced and kissed him." A divine encounter at the human level!

6. *Setting your sights.* Not only should the priority be right. The parent will find that the focus must be right. In that cold, pre-Passover night when Peter was warming himself, Jesus looked at him. The focus was correct, the soul was touched, and Peter came out of it just right.

What are *our* focal points: Baking cookies for the PTA? Washing clothes? Earning that extra dollar? Mending clothes? Do we overlook the main point? Or do we look straight into his or her eyes and say, "I am here, my child. I am really listening. Tell me your joys or problems."

A parent needs to put aside the busyness like Martha and focus on that particular moment when another opens his heart.

7. *Good focusing must become a habit.* The most important focal point of your child's life should be God. "Be still, and know that I am God," he says.

I have been practicing this kind of concentration for the past four years. It is not easy to "center down" on God. It takes

time and concentration, and I have failed many times. My mind
wanders. I get up at 5 A.M. every day. My body rebels and wants
to stay in the warm bed. But I groan and roll out.

I sit in a comfortable chair with the Psalms open before me
and read. I pray an old hymn such as:

Speak Lord in the stillness
While I wait on Thee:
Hushed my heart to listen
In expectancy.

Your concentration can be on only one center at a time, and it
takes practice to make it a habit. So pick a time when you
are alone. Empty your mind of every other thought.
Concentrate on the present. Absorb yourself completely in
what you are doing. Be completely open to the Spirit of
God. Visualize the face of Christ. Picture him at your side.
Sense inwardly his hand on your head. Speak his name over
and over. Slowly you will be aware of his presence. It is
hard for any of us to stay in such a moment long. But do it.
Practice it repeatedly when you are alone. He is there and
you will know it.

And *so is your child when he talks to you.* Try to be
completely his when he speaks. Surrender everything except
your dialogue with him. See him with a fresh vision. Immerse
yourself in the wonder of him as a child—a unique creation of
God. Only when you can open your mind to your child as he
blossoms are you seeing him as he truly is. Ask yourself some
pointed questions as you listen:

Who is this child of mine *really*?
Is my spiritual antenna tuned to him—am I hearing him?
How is he different from others?
In the immediacy of this moment, what is he like?
Have I heard him completely?
What has he really said as I listen with the "inner ear"?

Opening the window of your mind to your child should become
a habit. Real encounter with him will reward you as your
child becomes increasingly aware of your love. Obviously this

takes time and we do not always have as much as we would like. Martin Buber has taught us that the essence of our being is found in our relations to others. And Scripture says, "As we obey this commandment, to love one another, the darkness in our life disappears and the new light of life shines in."

8. *How often should this deep dialogue take place?* The more often we can do it the better. But doing it constantly is not a necessity. I remember my own dad winking at me across the dinner table occasionally when I was a boy. It was a wordless but meaningful small piece in a jigsaw of a larger encounter. Deeper dialogues took place once or twice a month.

A child does not need undivided attention. But when the parent *never* has time, the jigsaw of life cannot make sense. As long as your child has this concentrated attention occasionally, he can bear those moments when your attention must be somewhere else.

I have just returned from a visit to one of our orphanages in Colombia, South America. About two hours out of Bogotá in a little town named La Mesa, our houseparents are gathering children from death. One little boy, José, was on the verge of starvation. His mother had died of hunger just a few months before. José is now four, although he is only the size of a two-year-old. At first he kept wanting to go back to the place where he last saw his mother, hoping she would still be there.

It was hard even to put new shoes on him although his old ones were rags. He initially refused the new ones and took the old ones to bed with him. They were part of the "love jigsaw" that had previously made sense out of his life. He needed to reconstruct a life with his new parents. Making such a transition is heartbreaking for little children whose mother or father has been lost.

Often a crisis like this requires in-depth encounter for four to six months, followed by intermittent injections of demonstrated affection.

A child should be given focused attention particularly under pressure. It is good, as Dr. Hans Selye says, to check stress points and give an added measure of love during:

the death or departure of a parent
the arrival of a baby
starting school
moving to a new neighborhood
sudden losses
serious illnesses

At times like these a child's transition is smoothed by personal encounters. Depth touches are essential to his equilibrium. Let him look forward to these meetings to you by:

9. *Setting definite milestones for dialogue,* especially at those moments when your child will be facing great emotional pressure.

One of our houseparents in Korea sets a regular schedule for his children when he sees them approaching stress points. Each child gets a turn. I have watched him take a child on his lap and talk quietly of the child's daily experience:

"How did you do today?"
What were you happiest about?"
What made you angry?"
What did you dream about?"
Who did you play with?"

There are moments when he must correct. But too often we focus on a child's wrongdoing with a scolding. The child needs peaceful encounters too. Naturally the more he feels loved the better he will behave.

EXAMINE YOURSELF BEFORE DIALOGUE

If a parent leads a fulfilling life, he or she finds it easier to attend more directly to a child's hurts. Lack of self-fulfillment is an obstacle to having positive encounters with your child.

Martin Buber's concept "I-thou" has given rise to simple analogies. One is a fluorescent light having an anode and a cathode. "Relationships between two people," we may say, "are like a flash of light between two poles. The illumination that results is the true personhood of both poles. Personality is the light that joins two people." So it is with us and God. And so, too, it is with parent and child.

But when our mind is full of our own problems, the current is momentarily turned off, and we cannot communicate with the other. The tube goes dark and dialogue is broken.

When a father has a disappointed life, a shattered dream, he may tend to project an impossible dream on his son. But his dream may not be his child's.

Our ambitions for our youngster's future may blind us to the child's uniqueness. Accepting himself as he is will help a father to open out to his child unburdened by his own inadequacies.

Real dialogue is the powerful ingredient in projecting love to a boy or girl. "Little children," said the apostle John, "let us love one another, for love is of God."

But in order to love our child we must convince him that he rests safely in our care. In the next chapter we will consider ways in which a child can become aware of his safety with our love.

TWO
ESTABLISHING HIS SECURITY

"Don't be anxious about tomorrow. God will take care of your tomorrow" (Matthew 6:34, TLB).

No parent knowingly wants to cause his child anxiety. Nevertheless, anxiety shows up in many children.

It breaks one's heart to see a newly arrived child in one of our homes clinging to a chair because he does not trust people. A five-year-old with a "nervous breakdown"! An asthmatic seven-year-old! A ten-year-old girl with ulcers! A twelve-year-old who is promiscuous!

Often we don't realize that these and other symptoms abound in the child who feels unsafe. Most parents reject the notion that their child does not feel secure in their care. We tell ourselves:

"He gets three good meals a day!"
"We live in a good neighborhood."
"She goes to a nice school."
"I break my back to support him!"

But a child can often feel safe without many of these *things*. Jesus talks more about *soul-safety*. He tells about inoculations of love that are needed to prevent anxieties. A child often learns to erect a façade of indifference when love is missing. Inwardly he draws away from the parent as the prodigal did.

He articulates an "I don't care" attitude. He is on the road to the far country of distorted growth.

Only God is the perfect Parent. We humans are dim reflections of his fatherhood. He is *always* a safe refuge. We are limited ones. On the human level there is no perfect parent.

We fall short of the glory of God and his perfection, often injuring our loved ones. In the home we grate one another and cause abrasions. We don't like to admit it but it is true. Thankfully, given a modicum of love, our child can take it. He has been learning since babyhood.

"When should I start teaching Christianity to my child?" a parent asked a pastoral counselor.

"How old is your child?" he responded.

"Six months."

"Well, hurry home to him," he urged. "You have already wasted a half-year."

A child learns faith from the moment he is born. As he bursts into this strange new world, he asks,

"What is this dazzling place?"

"Am I safe here?"

"What are those noises?"

"Who are those strange creatures?"

"Can I count on them to help me?"

"Will they meet all my needs?"

"He is my place of safety," records the psalmist, "therefore in him will I trust."

Limited as we are, we parents must follow God's pattern. *Faith follows safety.* They are intermingled. "Can I trust him or her?" the child asks. If he cannot, he begins to sink into a quagmire of distrust that mars all future growth.

The pain-threshhold of a baby is low, and so is his discomfort level. Feeding the baby as he expresses hunger gives the child more than a full stomach. It communicates a sense of safety.

On St. Thomas Mount in Madras, India, I once watched a housemother tenderly holding a wizened baby. She was feeding her while humming a gentle song. The baby had been found on a trash heap crying weakly. I asked the houseparent about her feeding method. She nodded and said, "If we don't hold them and sing to them while we feed them, they often die."

Loving respect for the baby's ways and warm friendship lay foundations of faith. Easy relaxation with the infant creates a sense of safety. When a mother is a bundle of nerves, the baby gets the message and tenses up. When parents quarrel or have underlying disagreement it affects the infant's well-being. A mother will want to resolve these differences for her child's sake as well as her own.

The platform of faith has many planks. The answers to certain questions will tell us if we are laying them in place:

Does the child know where I am and when I will come back?

Do I avoid unexpected surprises?

Do I prepare him with confidence before a visit to the dentist or physician?

Have I gotten him ready psychologically for his first days at kindergarten or grade school?

Have I made promises I cannot keep?

There are scores of questions like this that will test the foundation of trust we are laying within him.

"THE CONFUSED REPORT SNARE" (THE HIDDEN MEANING)

Dr. Haim Ginott used to tell our classes at New York University about the mother who brought her troublesome son to him for counseling.

"First," she said, "I want you to understand that I love Joe even if he causes me heartache." With that she pursed her lips grimly and scowled at the boy.

She related various scrapes he had been in recently. Each episode concluded with, "It's a good thing I love him." A scowl would be repeated and her eyes would flash with anger.

Dr. Ginott anticipated the book *Body Language* and

cautioned us that our gestures, stance, and facial expression say far more than our words.

It is difficult for a child to discriminate between spoken words and underlying meanings as revealed by expressions and gestures. He is caught in the "confused report snare." He needs to decipher the true meaning of his mother's words versus her attitudes.

The Bible in Ephesians tells us to "speak the truth in love." Both truth and love must be balanced for full effectiveness.

Some years back I saw this illustrated in one of our Vietnamese homes. Minh Tan was a mischievous lad at a Nhatrang Orphanage where the superintendent Nguyen Sonh was trying "modern" Western methods of child care versus his Vietnamese upbringing. He had attended Iowa University and wanted desperately to be as "permissive" as he felt Iowa professors would advise. With this emotional conflict it is sometimes hard for Western-educated nationals to reenter their country's culture. He would smile when he saw misbehavior but would seethe inwardly. His behavior alternated between strict punishment and leniency. His uncertain message continually confused the children, sometimes resulting in schizoid behavior.

A child needs an honest statement of a parent's feelings. The "confused report" of the father or mother destroys a child's confidence and affection.

THE ONE MOST VITAL ELEMENT IS HONESTY

"What man is there of you whom if his son asks bread will give him a stone?" Jesus asked.

A child requires reality and honesty. We all remember the story of the emperor who wore fake clothing. It was a little child who discerned what the king really had on.

A little child is the most honest of God's creation. If he is having fun it is genuine. If he is miserable, it is clear to all. A child does not understand the subterfuge practiced by adults. Facts are facts. Feelings are feelings. This innocent honesty is commended by Christ. "Unless you become as a little child you cannot enter the kingdom of God." Because honesty makes a child feel safe, he can respond with like honesty.

WHY THE CONFUSED REPORT?

An adult gives a confused report in life for a variety of reasons:

Society is often dishonest and we fall into the same pattern.

Our fear of social disapproval causes us to dissimulate.

We feel that honesty sometimes makes us prey to being hoodwinked.

Our real feelings make us uncomfortable and we prefer to bury them under platitudes and clichés.

Being honest may often wound another person.

But especially with our children, dishonesty and subterfuge cause more ills than they cure.

One of our orphanage children in India came to us after her parents were killed in an accident. She was only four. The housemother said, thinking to ease her pain: "Your mother and daddy have gone on a long journey. But they will come back for you someday." The housemother felt the girl would be hurt by the news. But false hope eventually led to a childhood breakdown when Marnha was eight and discovered the truth.

Parents need to share their inner struggles with a child. The youngster can understand humanness better than dishonesty.

"Your mother and daddy have died and won't be back. They left me to be your mother," would have been a truer answer. It would have allowed Marnha to pour out grief and make a transition to the new parent. Loving care would have helped her bridge the gap, however painful.

A parent who nags constantly may be expressing much more than the immediate problem.

"You're always so sloppy," said one parent repeatedly. This adult had set impossible goals for that particular child and resented the shortcomings. The child saw only the nagging and felt that parental love was lessened.

Sharing these ambivalent feelings with the child helps.

"Jody, I have to tell you that I am angry with your sloppiness today. Something in me doesn't want to mention it. Another part of me resents your carelessness. I know that you are only a child and maybe I'm expecting too much."

By opening her conflicting feelings to Jody, the mother

displayed honesty. Most people are bundles of inner struggles and this is something a child can understand. But displaying only one feeling and hiding the other causes confusion in the child's emotions.

Often a parent may nag because he or she is tired and resents having to care for the child at that particular moment. The parent being irritable chooses a surface fault to camouflage the real resentment.

"You parents," says Ephesians, "don't keep on scolding and nagging your children, making them angry and resentful. Rather, bring them up with the loving discipline the Lord himself approves, with suggestions and godly advice" (6:4, TLB).

DOES HONESTY MEAN COMPLETE FRANKNESS?

The answer is no! There are some problems and emotions that are too heavy and are for adults only.

"When I was a child I spoke and thought and reasoned as a child does," says 1 Corinthians. "When I became a man my thoughts [and emotions] grew far beyond those of my childhood" (13:11, TLB).

Honesty in this instance can be expressed in such words as, "No, I'm not angry with you. But I'm upset about something that only an adult can understand." This is far preferable to telling the child there is nothing wrong and letting him worry about our unexplained emotion.

Whether to open up entirely, or how much to reveal of an adult emotion, must be determined by the parent. But even though we hold back details we should let the child know we are undergoing some sort of emotional struggle. This should not be camouflaged.

CAMOUFLAGING OTHER EMOTIONS

For some reason the evangelical world has looked askance at *anger* as one of the great sins—perhaps because it disrupts the smooth surface of the Christian community. Or perhaps because it connotes immaturity. In any case we tend to stifle it in the child, causing untold inner damage. Yet Scripture tells us, "If you are angry, don't sin by nursing your grudge."

Deep emotions are often hidden in the Protestant world, since they are thought of as not quite respectable. A male is taught to tamp down tenderness or grief. Stoicism is encouraged should he lose at sports.

Jack, a twelve-year-old in a Christian boarding school in India, was sent to his room in disgrace because he broke down and cried. Their team had just lost a cricket match. He was called a "sissy" by his classmates.

Our children have too often been taught, "It's wrong to have strong emotions. I must make believe that I do not have them."

A parent needs to lead his child to acknowledge that he has such feelings. He can encourage the youngster to share them when he needs to. The child must feel good about himself even when he has such inner surges since they are basic to all human reactions. Everyone has them constantly at various levels and they should be allowed to "ventilate."

When we as parents believe emotions are unreal, the child tries to emulate us. This causes him to downgrade himself when he discovers he does have strong emotions and falls short of the parental image.

Recently in an African orphanage the kitchen roof accidentally collapsed, causing a mild remark from the English headmaster. Henry, an eight-year-old, watched in surprise. Ordinarily he thought his own remarks would have been stronger.

"I guess it's not right to get excited," he decided. "I should make believe such things are normal."

On the other hand, a tense family conflict ending in a divorce should not make a child an emotional football. When such deeply trying times occur, the child in such a household should not be made to bear the burden of guilt, or fear, or hatred.

"Your father and I are getting a divorce," said one mother to her six-year-old. "I don't ever want to hear his name again!" This is too heavy a burden for a young child.

"Daddy and I are not going to live together anymore," would have been better. "Remember he loves you very much and so do I."

MIX FRANKNESS WITH TEMPERANCE

Let your child see your humanity. Certain parents feel they can never reveal weakness to their children. But we have already seen that God is the only perfect Parent.

"I'm never wrong about such things!" I heard one father tell his daughter. Later in her early adulthood I heard her throwing the phrase back at him. "I've heard you say that for twenty-three years!"

The parent who appears to be "perfect" is camouflaging and will be found out. A child needs a relationship with a genuine person. A parent to be human must admit his emotions. A child cannot deal with an automaton. A father or mother must be able to express phrases such as: "I'm tired." "I'm afraid." "I'm bewildered." "I'm worried." "I'm discouraged."

This does not deny any strength or worth in the parent. Indeed, it often requires courage to make such admissions. But it proves to the child that he can express his own feelings.

"Don't do that, dear," a mother told her boy who was beating a drum indoors. "Go outside and do it. I have a headache."

"Yes," said his five-year-old sister, "you're making me dizzy and nauseated."

One parent queried me, "Is it OK for me to tell my child I'm sorry when I've disciplined him by mistake?"

I well remember my own father apologizing to me years ago for a spanking I didn't deserve. My respect for him leaped light-years ahead and I reverence him to this day for his admission of weakness.

Children often surprise parents with their understanding and tolerance:

"That's all right, Mother. I knew you were tired that day," said one child.

It proves a magnet rather than a repellent for the child. A parent seems to them more human and tangible.

With his first child, George Brown felt that he should seem an all-wise father. He later felt less and less omniscient and increasingly relaxed. When he was unable to fix one of the first broken toys, he saw amazement in the child's eyes. He needed to explain that there were many things he could not do and a multitude of facts he did not know. After the shock, this allowed the youngster to admit her own shortcomings with a sense of security. If he had erected false façades, so would she. When he revealed his true self, "warts and all," the child relaxed and revealed her honest feelings.

Naturally, parental moods that swing unpredictably can be destructive to a child. One mother in a New York church I pastored had had a frightful background. Her parents had fought constantly and violently. She in later life, although functional in most instances, experienced wide ranges of moods. She could be optimistic and friendly one day and bitter and foreboding the next. Psychotherapy proved helpful to her and her children seemed to understand that she was coming to grips with her problem. This helped. But more especially when she faced real feelings, her children felt loved and reciprocated this affection. The family had a warmth that was lacking in more seemingly tranquil homes. Most important, the two children were freed from a sense of guilt knowing that their mother's emotions were not due to their misdeeds.

Faith and pride. When a child lives in an atmosphere of trust he can have pride in himself.

In 1966 I watched a group of our boys working in southern India. They were helping the headmaster carve laterite (a porous rock-like clay) from an embankment. When this substance is exposed to air and sunlight it hardens quickly into building blocks.

The boys (aged nine to thirteen) were building a cottage for their school complex. They worked quietly and confidently. Occasionally they looked at the headmaster observing his method. I took numerous photos of the lads laying block upon block. The headmaster rarely spoke, sometimes smiled encouragingly.

That must have been how Solomon's Temple grew, with little sound or turmoil. After four hours a half wall had risen. The self-satisfaction was apparent on each boy's face. Each felt his competence resulting from the trust of his headmaster.

Such mutual faith implies an acceptance—an ancient word almost synonymous with the word "grace." In the following pages let us examine the implications of an "accepting" parent and home.

THREE
ACCEPTING YOUR CHILD: GRACE

Through many dangers, toils and snares
I have already come;
'Tis grace hath brought me safe thus far,
And grace will lead me home.

To love a child is to accept him as he is. This is grace, and it is sometimes hard to practice—especially if you have a headache and he has a drum. Or if you want him to come in and he wants to stay out. It can test your powers of persuasive leadership.

Accepting the dirt and the deed while loving the child simultaneously is the measure of our grace. Leading him out of the deed and dirt can be the measure of our skill.

"I was a dirty little pickpocket," reports Park Woo Kwan, one of our Korea graduates. "I was found in a Seoul marketplace in 1952 with a dirty face and dirty little hands. I was a small wanderer, living in the trash heaps and doorways when I was finally caught by a policeman. He brought me to the Jae Il Children's Home. At first I didn't like the interference. But I discovered love there. My housemother was so patient with me. She washed me repeatedly and began the loving journey of teaching me right from wrong.

"They say that most children raised in orphanages have

defects because they lack love. But I never felt the lack of love. And I also learned the love of a kind American sponsor who helped me across the years and the miles. As a result of patient guidance, I was able to finish junior and senior high schools as well as college. Today I am a captain in the army appointed to lead a small mountain village near Taegu. This year I am starting my own business there. I am most especially grateful that my houseparent and my sponsor pointed the way to a living experience with Christ as Lord."

Park Woo went on to report that his "mother's discipline was never harsh." "Discipline," we remind ourselves, is derived from the word "disciple"—a learner or a follower —something that this young man absorbed through the years. The key to it was "the leading process." The housemother had learned to mellow in her discipline by unfolding inner grace or "acceptance"—which at last unraveled Park Woo's problem.

1. ACCEPTANCE OF YOUR CHILD WILL SET LIMITS

Scripture reminds us that we must "not sin that grace may abound." *Acceptance of the child* therefore *must set limits* on what he is allowed to do. Grace never means weakness, but is a tolerant way of living with a child.

Issa was a youngster in the Evangelical Home in Bethlehem who needed much of this kind of guidance. The wartime background of Israel during 1948 had caused him emotional disturbance. He was eight at the time and his father had died in the struggle. Thereafter, his mother had to work hard to support him. In 1950 she brought him to the Bethlehem residence, hoping that we would care for him. As Mr. Ghazaleh, the superintendent, told us, "It was a struggle to know when to apply pressure and when to be lenient. He was a fine-looking boy and everyone loved him. But his emotionalism caused him to run away repeatedly.

"Again and again he left the premises and our workers brought him back. Knowing his family problems, I myself often kept on my street clothes during the nighttime so that I could keep him from running away and being expelled. About four one morning I heard his window opening and caught Issa just before he jumped out. Through the years I helped keep him in school."

Haim Ginott writes that a child is more likely to accept limits when set by an outsider rather than a parent. This eventually proved true in Issa's case, for Mr. Ghazaleh with his firm love finally prevailed.

"Academically," he reports, "Issa was not very gifted. When he finished sixth grade, I sent him to our trade school, but emotional difficulties caused him to be put on probation. He ran away once more to his mother in Bethlehem at fifteen, and again I visited and counseled with him. His mother was very poor and not able to care for him. Reluctantly he returned with me and promised to work. But frankly I did not believe he could learn much. He was too hyperactive."

Mr. Ghazaleh at last found the realistic limits of Issa's ability and stress-threshold. His report concludes happily: "One day I noticed him carving a piece of olive wood and saw hidden talent. I urged him to work with a relative who had a woodcarving shop beside the Church of the Nativity. He began to do very good work and his products were soon being sold in Jerusalem and Bethlehem. In the early '60s he married and today all four of his children attend one of our day schools. Issa is now carving statues in stone and metal and his work is known everywhere."

Dr. Dana Farnsworth of the Harvard University Health Services examined the facts regarding young people like Issa, especially in those crucial teens. Based on a sampling of such teenagers he ascertained the following:

Out of 10,000 students about 1,000 have emotional conflicts of sufficient severity to warrant professional help.

100 to 200 were in the "I can't make myself work" state of apathy.

20 to 50 were so adversely affected by past family experiences that they were unable to control their impulses.

15 to 20 became ill enough to require treatment in a mental hospital.

And, sadly, 5 to 20 attempted suicide and one to three actually succeeded.

Some expected emotional causes were quarrelsome and broken homes, overprotective or excessively permissive homes. But the parents' part of the guilt ranged from *too little time to invest* in close companionship with their child to open or subtle pressure to fulfill the parents' own goal—not the child's.

Loving persistent guidance, setting reasonable limits, and providing a tolerant way of living with children can result in rich dividends. But this kind of "grace-full" acceptance requires strong mothers and fathers who have a keen sense of right and wrong and a willingness to seek the child's own aptitude levels and personal objectives.

2. ACCEPTANCE ALLOWS A CHILD TO ACT HIS AGE

The grace-full reception of a child means that we accept him because he is who he is, a growing human at a certain stage in his development. The parent will accept such behavior as is right, natural, and healthy for a child of that age.

It was love like this that won the heart of Elizabeth McDonald, who grew up in our girls' home in Madras. Her mother and father, Anglo-Indians, had died in the turmoil for Indian independence, and she was found wandering the streets. Brought into the home at age six, she proved to be a lively and imaginative addition. Her pranks were always good-hearted, but it took patient understanding on the part of houseparents, especially when jokes occurred at inopportune moments. "Whenever there was noise and laughter in the home," said one of the older workers, "we knew that Elizabeth was at the center of it."

I asked this staff person how she coped with Elizabeth's high spirits. "I just expected her to be a child—not an angel," she said.

She was always an integral part of the warm home climate as she grew, and had a natural aptitude with people. Her academic grades were high, and the institution was able to arrange for a scholarship to business college in England. Graduating with honors, she was soon proving herself in the British business world. Rather rapidly she accumulated a small fortune, but in her early thirties was tragically killed in an accident.

In her will, she left the home a generous bequest to build a chapel and parish home. The words in the will were moving ones: "In appreciation for my housemothers who were so patient on those days when I was impossible!"

The good parent finds it possible—even pleasant—to coexist with noises of childhood. In fact, if the child is to be normal, the parent *must* learn to so live with such standard behaviors that each age level may unfold gracefully. Saying yes to the child at the right moment allows him not only the additional satisfaction of making his own decision, but also of enjoying our faith in him.

Dag Hammarskjold carries this to a personal affirmation of the child at the infinite level in his *Markings:* "I don't know who or what put the question. I don't know when it was put. But at that same moment I did answer 'Yes' to God. And from that moment I was certain that my existence was meaningful and that, therefore, my life in full surrender had a goal."

3. ACCEPTANCE ALLOWS FOR A CHILD'S CURIOSITY

The Gospel of Luke seems to emphasize the manner in which little children clustered around Jesus. They were curious and excited about this wonderful and gentle Man.

In order to grow in thought and knowledge, the child must be exposed to varieties of sensory experiences. I have watched with interest in five continents as our workers provide for this child-need.

In one of our Chinese homes for the handicapped, chairs and tables and wallboards have been specially designed in proper proportions. The children are given the opportunity to work with their hands, touching, tasting, asking, and seeing. As a result children like Nung Shiu Jean learn to cope at early ages.

Nung grew up in our Bethany Home. Nothing was known about his mother and father, but when he came to us he had already suffered the ravages of polio. The home provided most of the things available in normal homes. When he was fourteen, he was even a star player on the home's basketball team, despite his twisted legs. He early showed an aptitude with his hands and a particular skill in leathergoods. An apprenticeship for two years in a shoe company was arranged so that he could learn the trade. Now in his twenties, Nung has his own shoe company which is showing a satisfactory profit. The opportunity to experiment and choose had been a vital element in his growth.

Dr. Teofilo Santi, of the Casa Materna Home in Italy, told us about one boy named Giorgio who came to them as a lad of five. His mother was a refugee from Hungary who died of malnutrition just before Giorgio came to the institution. Giorgio himself had tendencies to tuberculosis and needed constant care and therapy. It was clear that the best environment for him would be in an outdoor vocation. From his boyhood, therefore, he insisted on working in Casa Materna's gardens.

"It's so wonderful to work with the flowers and bees and ants!" he said.

It was in this setting that he first gave his heart to Christ in thanksgiving for the beauty of creation. As the boy grew, Dr. Santi was able to steer Giorgio's learning experiences into botany and entomology. When he was seventeen, he entered the Agricultural College at Formia. On his vacations he often brought seeds home to plant in the Casa Materna gardens.

Today he is twenty-five, married, and lives in Germany, where he works in Munich's public gardens. Because his early choices were respected, Giorgio has found a deeply satisfying life.

A Harvard dean once said, "If parents can just be quiet and listen, the child will ultimately make good sense to himself."

When a child can question and experiment with the unknown, this will be the basis for his advancement. When a parent tries to stamp out such experimental qualities (present in every baby) he is holding back the child's progress. Each parent is responsible for keeping alight the lamp of curiosity. Every youngster must know that there are rich dividends in wondering. His quest for knowledge should be part of his self-esteem.

4. ACCEPTANCE MEANS THAT WE MUST OFTEN BE WILLING TO TOLERATE BEHAVIOR THAT IS NOT GROWN-UP

At certain age levels it is essential that the child be allowed his noise and boisterousness. Se Jung Rin ("Jimmy") was an example of that. Born before the Korean war, he was cast on his own early in life. His father had been killed in the first attack on Seoul and his mother was separated from him in the endless refugee lines. He was one of the multitude of ragged boys and girls who roamed at will, begging and pilfering.

For a time he entered one of the many orphanages that dotted Korea during and after the conflict. But his high spirits and independence caused some disruption and the superintendent was impatient, forcing the lad back onto the streets once again. He became one of the tough little guys who could outdrink, outsmoke, and outswear all the others. But one day his mother found him wandering the darkened streets. She took him lovingly but firmly in hand. A dedicated Christian, she never ceased to pray for Jimmy. Every morning she arose at 4:30 before work and prayed diligently for her son and his spiritual awakening. Because of war privations, she did not live to see his conversion.

After her death, Jimmy entered the Korean army and after several years was sent to Indochina to serve with the Allied forces. While on duty in Saigon the Lord met him forcefully and saved him. Erik Erikson (in *Childhood and Society*) explains this phenomenon by saying, "The mother's face, her arms, her breast are the child's first geography. And to this he always somehow returns."

As a karate expert and skydiver, Jimmy was admirably suited for the army. But after his discharge he found that his early street life had prepared him to work with legions of ragged tots that swarmed the city streets of Phnom Penh. With his skimpy savings he started an orphanage and gathered several hundred boys and girls. He rented an old farmhouse on the outskirts of the Cambodian capital for ten dollars a month. There, with his own hands, he constructed beds which were crude platforms covered with straw mats. He set up classes for the youngsters and found Cambodian teachers to help him. One by one he led each child to Christ.

In commenting to me about his exciting biography, he said, "My mother's patience and prayers through all my scrapes brought me to him!"

The parent needs to be ready for the various stages of the child in which he alternates in behavior patterns. The firm but loving understanding of Christ with Mary Magdalene, Zaccheus, and the Samaritan woman indicates the divine pattern a parent can follow even in extremes. Stubbornness, sloppiness, slowness can all be tolerated when the parent knows this will surely be on his child's growth track.

By accepting Jimmy's feelings while not accepting his deeds, his mother had left an open door. It is increasingly easy for a mother to do this when she does not judge him by her own emotions but beholds her child as an entirely separate person. But there can be no counterfeit acceptance. If it is to be helpful to the child, it must be real.

5. ACCEPTANCE DOES NOT MEAN HARSHNESS

Scripture says, "He that controls his own spirit is greater than he that rules a city." It is fruitless to attempt controlling another before one's own temper has been brought under proper rein.

Expression of uncontrolled anger may be a release to the parent, but it never benefits the child. Such outbursts often indicate severe neurosis or borderline psychosis. One case cited from the court reads:

"The mother brought the child to the doctor's office at which time she was unconscious with obvious brain or spinal injuries. The child died shortly thereafter and an autopsy was performed, revealing several lacerations of the brain which were caused by distinct traumata to the head. The mother stated that she punished the child several times by hitting her head against the wall. But she said that the child had 'fallen off the bed' just before she brought the youngster to the physician this time. Neighbors said that they had witnessed severe whippings by the mother."

Such parents themselves need therapy, and often the children should be removed until the adult involved is declared normal.

I have listed a series of guidelines indicating negative qualities that would preclude hiring improper houseparents for our children:

"Is the parent ego-centered?"
"Does he have a negative attitude?"
"Is he a fault-finder?"
"Is he too timid?"
"Is he uncooperative?"
"Is he a poor model?"
"Does he have any moral problem?"
"Is he emotionally unstable?"
"Does he exploit children for self-gain of any kind?"
"Does he use harsh discipline?"
"Is he indifferent to a child's emotional problems?"

Thomas Gordon has said that there are three ways to set limits: Keep your power; give your power away; or share your power. The procedure we use as parents will decide who sets limits in our family and how they are administered.

Unfortunately the idea of sharing power is beyond many of us. Power is too often something we need to enhance our self-image. Being able to control another, no matter how young, makes us feel important.

The oldest method is that of the authoritarian. The Old Testament proverb of "spare the rod—spoil the child," needs interpretation. "Children should be seen, not heard," was common in my own childhood. It is the parent who must make the decision on this.

There is a difference between authoritarianism and authority. Authoritarianism is often based on physical strength. Authority is based on parental competence. It is the latter that will reach into the heart of the child.

If the child is made to feel that his parent *always* knows best, his own self-confidence is diminished. He becomes a "second-class citizen" in his own home. He cannot grow into full maturity and self-respect. The authoritarian parent depends on *outward* conformity, but often the child boils inwardly.

Obviously there are times when a parent must say no. But even then, listening to the child with empathy is vital to the youngster's self-respect. Hearing his disappointments, his frustrations, or even his anger toward our discipline helps him to ventilate his feelings and to grow as a person.

Conversely, when a child is treated unfairly the time will come for retribution. Such a young life will begin to hit back as he grows. He will strike out at a world that he feels has not been good to him. Poor behavior grows in soil like this, while love will fertilize maturity.

6. ACCEPTANCE MEANS CREATING A WORLD IN WHICH THE CHILD CAN BE COMFORTABLE

Obviously the word "comfortable" does not necessarily mean physical comfort. But it does mean allowing the child to act his age so that he will not have to come back later and relive that age. At eight or eighteen he does not have to live like a two-year-old because he was allowed to act like a two-year-old at that chronological point in his life.

Ahn Jong was forced by circumstances and unfeeling adults into such a predicament. His parents were killed during the Korean war and he was swept onto the streets of Wonju. There at the age of six, he was found by a friendly GI and brought to the Cha Shin orphanage.

The superintendent took a warm interest in the children. But Ahn Jong was a problem child, and his street habits caused him to be expelled along with some other boys. They begged on the streets for several months until hunger drove them back to Cha Shin. The father of the home forgave them and warmly reinstated them. But Ahn Jong, because of his troubled childhood, did not readily overcome some of his bad habits.

"In later life," he tells us, "I became insolent and greedy, and God had to correct me many times. Finally with his help I found a good wife and was able to settle down. Today I have three little sons and a daughter. I am so grateful to my housefather for the patience he had during my formative years. He received me back, just as the parable father opened his arms to the prodigal. And even today he gives me wise advice, although he is now very elderly."

Acceptance of the child allows the child with loving firmness to grow up at his own pace. Although years are often consumed, he blooms into more self-control, better judgment, and sweet reason.

7. ACCEPTANCE MEANS THAT THE PARENT AND CHILD CAN LIVE AND WORK TOGETHER IN PEACE AND HAPPINESS

When a child is truly accepted, the mother does not need constantly to fight to make the child act like an adult. Nor does the child need to fight any longer to be himself. Sometimes this is hardest when a child is handicapped in some way, and the parent finds it difficult to accept the handicap. For the child, nonacceptance can have a devastating effect. This can happen, too, when parents are absent.

Hwang Jae too was a war orphan in Korea, from Kodong Island, in 1951. He was only three at the time, had been an only son of two very loving parents. Sadly they were killed in the first year of the conflict and their home was reduced to splinters. The boy's grandfather, although elderly, took care of him until he was six. It was then that a bomb fell on their house; the grandparent was killed instantly and Hwang Jae was permanently blinded.

"How helpless I was—and how much in pain! But God did not forsake me. When I received Jesus into my heart, I realized God's overriding will was intended to show his glory through me, a totally blinded person.

"An American chaplain led me to the Taegu Lighthouse, a home for blind children. Here I was given a golden opportunity to study and learn a life-skill.

"Gradually I was able to forget the sorrow of losing my parents and grandfather. Through the years I was consoled by learning skills on several musical instruments—trumpet, piano, and organ. The Lord opened doors so that I could play concerts at many churches throughout the country, and the proceeds were used to build schools for other handicapped children."

Today he is married and the father of one son. His gratitude is evident in his final words, "I am thankful for the patient guidance through the years. I believe I am now charged by God to devote my life to help other handicapped children like me."

The child who can say to himself concerning his parents, "They are good to me, they understand me," has a priceless gift. More lessons in good living seep into the child's bloodstream twenty-four hours a day than could ever be spanked or yelled into him. A child learns to imitate his parent. And for the parents, Paul says, "Be ye imitators of God as dear children."

8. ACCEPTANCE DOES NOT MEAN THERE WILL NEVER BE DISCIPLINE

Limits on behavior are essential to the child's growth. Kindness is only one element in producing good behavior. A loving parent expects his child to act his age. This means the youngster should act *up to* his age—not like a baby. Clear messages on right and wrong should be in the child's daily curriculum at home and at school.

In his early life Park Jun did not have the advantage of such steady moral guidance. His father had been a school teacher but was captured by the North Koreans and never heard from again. Park's mother worked as a housemaid to support her little son, but the wages were pitifully inadequate. Moreover, she had little time to devote to her youngster. He ran the streets of Jae Ju without much control.

The table was always meagerly set. "We were too poor to buy rice," he recalls, "and had to fill our stomachs with wheat husks, normally fed to pigs. There was no money for me to attend school, and we could not afford textbooks. So I ran around with the bad boys of the schools, gambling and stealing from small shops. Nevertheless my mother constantly reminded me of my father's profession as a schoolteacher years before—and what a proud calling it was. That was what repeatedly brought me back again. However there was still no money for me to continue school.

"About then my mother learned about a school connected with the widows' home in Jaeju. We were so hungry and desperate that we swallowed our pride and asked if we could be admitted. They opened their doors warmly to us and gave us not only a home but daily bread and the opportunity for me to return to school. That week I was led to Jesus and converted from a thief to a Christian boy. God did supply small funds for my schooling.

"But as I continued in public high school, I often was reminded of how poor I was. I had to save in every way possible. I used scrap paper for my notes. I washed my face with a cup of cold water in the mornings. I could not afford a school bag so I wrapped my ragged books and pencils in cloth.

"Once I was punished in high school because I wore black rubbers rather than gym shoes. But I simply didn't have the money for such luxuries.

"At nineteen I began to teach primary school and made it a rule to deposit two-thirds of my salary in the bank. I was also able to help needy neighbors with one-tenth of my savings. God has aided me in sending eleven boys and girls to school thus far, and I hope for more."

In recalling his experience, Park remembers that his mother's love and the superintendent's steady hand made the difference in his life.

Park's mother and houseparent used at least four approaches to discipline methods that produced good results: through reasoning and guidance; occasionally through punishment melded with love; through making Park feel comfortable with his parents and a knowledge that they were comfortable with him; through a genuine joy that Park was their child.

9. ACCEPTANCE MEANS CHANNELING A CHILD'S BEHAVIOR INTO ACCEPTABLE ACTIVITIES

The parent must say from time to time, "It's all right for you to play that drum—but not in here!" Or one might say, "It's OK for you to ride your bicycle, but not now!" Or occasionally a mother might say to her little girl, "You can play dress-up —but not with *my new clothes!*"

The parent is not afraid to say no when the situation demands.

Oh Sung, by his own admission, was a "mischievous problem child" at the An Hung orphanage. "I came to the home when I was nine years old. For a long time after I arrived, my days were filled with wrongdoing. Along with the children of my own age, I sneaked into the nearby orchards stealing sacks of fruit. We would hide them in a convenient spot and enjoy them at leisure.

"From fruit we branched out into chickens. During the winter months we would hunt for fat hens in the neighbors' yards. I would bait a hook with fat pieces of corn and throw a line over the fence. Sooner or later a foolish hen took the bait and several of us quickly pulled the line (and hen) to a safe spot. An open-air fire quickly turned the bird into a delicious afternoon snack."

The housemother's discipline was never long in coming, and Oh's acts ended in discomfort. "I was kept in the teachers' lodge until twilight that day and had to eat barley rather than rice for supper. I remember praying, 'Lord, you promised to answer all our prayers. Now I pray that you make this barley into rice.' But when I opened my eyes, the barley was still there. I was really beginning to doubt the power of prayer and all promises in the Bible. But my housemother remained loving and kind throughout it all. How often she prayed with me.

"It was not long until high school days, when I found God was really answering prayers, and slowly my faith returned. I began in my third year to pray that God might send me to college. A friend of mine gave me an application and urged me to sit for the entrance examinations. I did not regard this as total answer to prayer or even a possibility until I received a cable saying that I had passed with high grades and that World Vision would supply a scholarship. I can still remember my joy and prayer at that moment, 'O Lord, how I thank you! Someday I will surely repay your blessing by helping another unfortunate youngster.'

"Although I had a scholarship, I was still very short of money and had to sleep in empty classrooms at night. I sold Christmas cards in winter and did construction work in summer. Because of sleeping outside, often in snow and dew, I contracted pleurisy. But God was still good to me. Peter Lee, a child care director for Korea, found a bed for me at the Children's Clinic, and in three months I was well again.

"Finishing college, I was admitted to the army, working to become a commissioned officer. Unfortunately, I did not pass the officers' requirements and was bitterly disappointed. But again the Lord had something better for me, for I was assigned as an assistant to the Army chaplain. There he provided me with many precious hours for prayer and study. After my discharge, I went on to graduate school for a master's degree. Once more, God supplied resources and an opening for me to attend Theological Seminary in South Carolina.

"Looking back on my past thirty years, I find that they have been mingled with corrections, hardships, and ordeals. But each time an ordeal appeared, I was given courage and an open door for new opportunity."

Robert Raines' beautiful prayer puts it best:

Father
shield the children from my weaknesses
protect them against my attempts to
round them off or square them away . . .

let me understand them when they are
bearing burdens they cannot share with me
nor let me help carry . . .

let me not pry when I see them suffering
from sins unpublished
but deep with inner shame . . .

let them be brave and safe
but if they cannot be both
let them be brave . . .

let me share their tiny tragedies
and terrible heartaches
their soaring delights and
silent revelations
if they want me to
and as they want me to . . .

let their confidence be established in
you . . .

Having thus examined some of the ways a parent can accept his child, we need next to turn to the child's self-acceptance. I have termed this "inward grace" and we will attempt to deal with it in the following chapter.

FOUR
HELPING HIM ACCEPT HIMSELF: INNER GRACE

Lee Kyung Ja was one who felt rejected by her natural parents and as a result found it hard to accept herself. She was troubled by a festering resentment toward them through the years.

Most parents want their child to be "well-adjusted." But to reach this goal, the child needs to have a sense of realism, to take into account all facts before he embarks on a course of action. He must feel at ease in criticizing his own path of activity at any time. And he should be well aware that there will be a price to pay, should he be careless or thoughtless in pursuit of his objective. But he must first feel secure in a parent's love.

"I do not even know my exact name or birthdate," related Lee Kyung, "I do not remember what my parents were like because they left me on the doorstep of the Soon Zul Babies Home when I was an infant. An artificial name and birthdate were given to me by my superintendent. When I was seven, I was sent to another orphanage named Wonju Shin and there I began to attend primary school. But always there was a seed of anger in my heart that my parents should have abandoned me. All the other children looked happy and contented while I felt so miserable.

"As I grew older, the resentment grew so great that I began to lose interest in everything I was doing. The first symptom of this was neglect of my studies. Days and nights were simply spent in bitterness for my nameless parents. Repeatedly I wondered why they allowed me to be born into this world, when they were not willing to bring me up properly. I spent night after night crying into my pillow. Eventually I dropped out of senior high school, although my housemother tried to persuade me to remain.

"After that, the superintendent gave me the supervision of gardening and sewing at the home. But my housemother kept at me and finally persuaded me to attend the vocational school. Finally when I was at an all-time low, I met Christ. The quality of my work improved after that, and I was able to find a job as a dressmaker. Slowly I reconciled myself to life *as it was*, with the love of my houseparents and friends."

Lee Kyung did emerge beautifully, undergirded by affectionate esteem from her small but warm community. In being self-accepting, she became willing to commit all of her energies to her dressmaking, even though she knew it might fail. A child must value his goal so much that the possibility of gaining will outweigh the risk of failure. With a consistent set of aims he will have a road he can productively follow.

1. THE SELF-ACCEPTING CHILD HAS FAITH IN HIS ABILITY TO COPE WITH LIFE

When a youngster feels like a "flop," he tends to fail at parties, to be shy and self-effacing. He may walk and talk contrary to the way he does in school or church. Grownups are the same. There is always the man who is self-assured and vocal in professional surroundings. But at parties he has two left feet. The wider a child's areas of competence, the greater his total confidence.

Hyun Dae was five years old when he was abandoned by his mother in a small Song Jung restaurant. His mother gave him some cookies and said she would be right back. But he never saw her again. "I remember crying and crying," he recalls. "I finally crept under the table and slept there all night. When the owner found me next morning, he was very kind. That day he took me to the social welfare center and from there to Kangjin orphanage."

But such rejection has its lasting effect. Hyun told himself that he was not very important if his mother could leave him like that. From that developed more inner failures. He felt he could not do things as well as others. He felt there was no use in attempting novel things. He did not think he could succeed and was indecisive about even small choices. He remained mute because he believed he had nothing to say worth hearing.

The turning point in his life was an American "sponsor" who wrote to him and sent gifts. "Through her letters I felt a 'mother's' love for me although I never met her in person."

"I felt," he said, "as though I had become a real member of a home when I opened my first package from her, and I could have real confidence in everything. I was influenced very much by this Miss Kery, who encouraged me to be a faithful man. What precious help I received from her!

"I finished my courses in primary and secondary schools and then went on to agricultural college. Today I am working at the Agricultural Bank in Kangjin."

The turning point in such a child's life comes when he can say, "I think I can do something that is of value to others. My parents or loved ones feel that I am worth respecting. I can't do everything well, but I do have a number of things of which I can be proud. I realize that I do not know everything, but I can and will learn more. If I don't first succeed, I will try again. I can be happy in the company of others, but I can also be satisfied alone. I always have some valuable thing to do. I am happy because I am almost always comfortable with myself."

2. THE SELF-ACCEPTING CHILD CONSIDERS HIMSELF EQUAL TO OTHERS

The youngster who has inner feelings of inadequacy sometimes tries to compensate by appearing overly confident outwardly. But the child who believes he has strong capabilities within himself, does not feel obligated to appear excessively assured on the outside.

A Pueblo Indian grandmother once told Dr. Robert Coles:

"When you go to our children, try to become a friendly tree that they will want to sit near. Enjoy them. Forget yourself. If we could all forget ourselves a bit more—then our children would feel free to be a bit more themselves. Sometimes we get too close to our children. We scare them with ourselves. They can't then become themselves. It is *them* we should try to know."

What the child needs is to learn to smile and to laugh, to be angry and to be mischievous within reason—all of these he should have to gain inward integrity.

When a child expects to be a winner, his chances of being victorious soar geometrically. If he anticipates being a loser, his whole body will agree and will help him fail. The youngster must have faith in himself in order to succeed.

Solomon was one such youngster we worked with who was burdened with a sense of foreboding that he could not enter college. Our houseparent finally asked him to sit down and make a list of his past successes for that month. Laboriously he jotted them down:

"Scored high in football this week."
"Got good grades in math during this month."
"Learned five Bible verses."
"Made my bed every day this month before classes."
"Learned to jump an inch higher in gym class."

The parent then asked him to read this list over and recall the good feeling he had after each success. "Try," he exhorted, "to remember the happiness and 'success taste' that made each victory possible." Every review of this list left him with greater courage to face his college entrance exam. Somehow, too, he seemed to have more *energy* to study for the tests and more ambition to try each new problem, as he pored over his books.

Solomon had been a poor gypsy boy of six, ragged and undernourished, when he was left at the door of one of our Bombay homes. His mother had apparently died and his father had remarried. The new mother would not accept the youngster. It was this sense of being unwanted that had flooded over him periodically and had given him a sense of defeat. "But he graduated with flying colors," reported the superintendent, "and easily passed his college entrance tests.

Today he is completing his theological training to become
a minister. His smaller successes led him on to ever greater
ones."

A child's whole life-pattern can be different when he has
great self-respect. His attitudes, play-habits, conversation,
work, and even the way he walks reflect the fact that he
likes himself. There is about him an aura of inward assurance.
As he grows he becomes increasingly able to cope with
daily problems. He develops into a creator out of this nucleus
of self-confidence.

3. THE SELF-ACCEPTING CHILD DOES NOT FEEL HE IS ABNORMAL

Our mental institutions are loaded with children and adults
who have developed distorted inner pictures of themselves.
Instead of thinking positively about themselves, life has taught
them to think negatively. This usually grows out of a home
life that has shattered or distorted a child's image of normality.
The youngster can learn unwholesome defenses or he may tend
to withdraw when faced with twisted parental images. By
thwarting self-respect we can squelch healthy development.
Worse than that, we can actually nurture warped progress in
the youngster.

Yoo Sung experienced such warping as he grew. He was
born during the Korean war and never knew his parents. A
kindly stranger brought him to the Hong Ik Home on Cheju
Island. Here he was treated warmly, but being an orphan was a
cause for ridicule by public school companions. From
the first grade on he felt the stigma that Far East culture often
attaches to parentless children. This continued through his
primary and secondary training days and even into his
apprenticeship.

The housefather had seen his particular skill in electronics
and had put him into a shop as a journeyman. But the stigma
followed him there also. The teacher joined in the derision
with words such as, "You are nothing but an orphan—an
ill-natured oaf who eats too much boiled rice." Eventually the
pressure of the boys and the teacher forced Yoo Sung out
into the streets again.

He struggled to survive and often had to stay on the streets at night with little to eat. Finally, after much prayer, he appealed to his old housefather who received him back into the orphanage. The parent lovingly encouraged him to study for a civil service exam. With reminders of past successes and emotional undergirding, Yoo Sung passed the examination and today is an official in Korea's forestry department.

When a child is valued by both family and society, his play and work can be nondefensive. He does not need to use his vitality to protect himself. With his guard down, he can make friends more easily, put his full energy into study, and relax in class. Surrounded by a benevolent climate he can move into ever-widening circles of achievement. He feels normal and accepted by himself and others.

4. THE SELF-ACCEPTING CHILD IS NOT SHY OR SELF-CONSCIOUS

When a child feels he cannot be loved this is like having blinders that shut out his own lovable qualities from his inner eye. He will discard views that do not match his distorted picture of himself. A child normally has a coherent image of who he is, in harmony with other people's views of him.

One boy came to a Middle Eastern home from an unhappy family life. He had been downgraded by both mother and father since birth because he was an unwanted child. Eventually the father brought him to one of our homes with the shocking remark, "We don't want him—he's too ugly!" He was only four, but he had been badly damaged by this constant rejection.

Far from being ugly, Ibrahim was handsome, with large brown eyes and tight curly hair. But the houseparents had difficulty getting his clothes off him at night, he was so stiff— almost catatonic. For a while he seemed to have autistic problems—making only small moaning sounds. In time, he regained his speech ability under loving care by the staff. He quickly became a great favorite in the home. But his hunger for love and approval were touching. In my mind's eye I can still see him at age five standing at the top of a flight of stairs pleading, "Take me home with you. Please take me home!"

It took much patience and understanding through the years, but as he grew, Ibrahim became increasingly self-accepting.

Today at twenty he is a craftsman in Nazareth, married and the loving father of a baby girl.

Unfortunately there is the child who can only see repulsion in every gesture of an adult. We all know the youngster who cringes whenever his parent raises a hand. Even more damaging is the tot who cringes inwardly at every word and communication from the adult world. He expects himself to fail and thus always does things that will insure such failure. And whenever there is a change in such a child's circumstances, he always expects the worst.

On the other hand, there is the child who has supportive parents. He has learned to strain out every negative thought about himself so that he can see himself in a positive light. When parents and teachers can provide a nurturing climate, a child can change negative views of himself to self-affirming ones. But there is the youngster who does not adapt easily when the emotional atmosphere changes. His negative self-image is set in concrete. How important then, for a child to experience warm acceptance from early infancy.

5. THE SELF-ACCEPTING CHILD FOLLOWS HIS OWN STANDARDS AND IS NOT SWAYED BY THE CROWD

The firmer a child's feelings of personal value, the more self-assured he is in a group situation, and the more easily he bases his actions on personal judgments. Although he likes it, he does not nourish himself on group approval. He has a realistic view of his own shortcomings as well as his own convictions. Such convictions grow out of cordial and affirming experiences in early life with the parent.

Such training stayed with one of our boys named Jang Chan. His father had been a pastor in Korea when the war broke out. But sadly, the day after the war began his little town was destroyed by bombs. "When my sister and I came home from school, there was fire everywhere. Our house was just not there—only a hole in the ground remained. Mother and father were gone forever.

"We were terribly hungry when someone put us on a bus for Taegu and gave us a few coins. With the money I bought some candy and gum and sold it to GIs on the streets. The proceeds gave us enough to eat, but my sister and I had nowhere to sleep. So we gathered sticks of wood and made a shack near the Taegu YMCA."

One night a thief broke into their shack and stole their meager possessions. The experience crushed them, and Jang Chan stopped praying. He was tempted to enter the life of thievery himself, but his parents' strong influence held him back.

Soon he and his sister were discovered by a missionary and taken to the So Mang orphanage in Taegu. They both settled into the routine life easily. The sister began taking an interest in hairdressing. And Jang Chan became a dedicated student. After college, he was hired by a leading book publisher, and today he manages an important branch office in Seoul. Needless to say, his spiritual life has deepened in the experience.

A child with such a background resists the drive to steal from or cheat another. His strongly entrenched "inner parent" tells him that he is only cheating himself. Interestingly, he does not even feel that he has made a great moral choice. His entire early conditioning and his religious community have made the choice for him. This can only occur, however, when the convictions have been nurtured in a warm and loving atmosphere at an early age.

6. THE SELF-ACCEPTING CHILD CAN TAKE PRAISE OR BLAME WITHOUT CONCEIT OR HUMILIATION

Good self-acceptance is not loud braggadocio. It is a calm awareness of self-respect and pride. Such a child values himself for what he is and is happy to be himself. Braggadocio on the other hand is usually a screen to hide a sense of personal worthlessness. The self-accepting child doesn't need to spin his wheels or blow his horn to prove his worth. He already is well aware of it.

Just such a person was Basil in our Evangelical Home in Ramallah. He lost his father when he was only one. His young mother then had two children, Basil and Hanna. She brought them both to the evangelical day nursery at first, while she studied nursing and became a midwife. In the evenings she impressed them with the importance of an education.

"You can do anything you want," she told Basil, "as long as you work hard and study."

He remembered when she had first said that, although he had been only two-and-a-half at the time. He and Hanna could read the Bible even before they went to formal grades. The mother's loving ambition for him eventually sent him to a Christian boarding school in Lebanon. He completed his primary and secondary education in this eighty-year-old Christian institution and made application to a college in Germany. Backed by funds from his industrious mother and some friends, he finished his medical training and is now a skilled surgeon. He plans to return within five years to build a small hospital for his people in Beit Sahour, so that he can serve his country and his Lord. When asked if he ever had doubts about his ability to reach his goal, he said:

"No. My mother believed in me. So I believed in myself."

Self-regard, or lack of it, from early childhood, imprints a child for life, either tracing his way to success or to failure. The parent must emblazon in his youngster a thoroughgoing belief in himself, so that he can move successively through the obstacles of life. Dr. Paul Tournier tells us, "Behind every word and attitude a person is able to distinguish that secret and incessant bracing of one's self and reputation." And Pascal says, "We move continually to adorn and preserve one's imaginary self."

7. THE SELF-ACCEPTING CHILD DOES NOT CONDEMN HIMSELF IF HE CANNOT PERFORM CERTAIN SKILLS

Nor does he deny his superior qualities. Each youngster searches for a way to have a good inner picture of himself. And with that he attempts to match the portrait with his actions. Some, of course, are not so successful. When he is certain about himself, a child can make unhesitating statements. When he is not, he often stammers.

Montaigne, the great essayist, remarked, "Only you yourself know whether you are cowardly or brave; others do not see you; they make only uncertain conjectures about you. They do not see so much your actual self as your self-revelation."

Dhan Sripur tells of his struggle with this problem. He did not know much about his early childhood, but he remembers wandering through the Indian streets begging with his small bowl. Older boys beat him repeatedly and stole his rice. "I did not feel worth much," he confesses. But when he was about six, a pastor saw him at the railway begging and brought him to a home in Nagpur.

The pastor demonstrated love for Dhan from the beginning. But the other children did not accept him readily. One day when he returned from school he says, "I found two things that made me sad and discouraged. One was that my favorite toy was broken. The second was that I was surrounded by boys twice my size. They did not like me and beat me again and again. I did not know what to do for I did not want to tattle on them. I knew that the pastor loved us all. So I turned more and more to God. When they beat me, I went secretly to the chapel where I talked to God and sang hymns. That was always a comfort. I was unfortunately never very good at games or in handcrafts.

"As I grew I became aware that God wanted me to tell people about him and his love. It was then I decided I must go to seminary when I was bigger. About then I was given a World Vision sponsor who took great interest in me. Eventually he sent me money for schooling and my prayers came true. When I was a sophomore in Bible college I became an evangelist for a church with 200 members. When I graduated they made me the pastor.

"Now we have many services and more people. We have early morning prayer meetings and many Bible study groups.

"I had a growing feeling through my boyhood and youth that this was what he wanted. I soon learned that I could not compete with others in many things. There was really only one thing I could do well—preach about him and worship him."

The child will often push himself rigorously in his areas of strength, when he knows there is no hope in others. Psychologists call this *compensation* and it is one of the devices a child must use to build his self-esteem. A parent can discuss such constructive methods with the youngster, showing him alternatives to his weaker areas.

When a child feels he is a failure in one thing, this simply adds to his defeat in other fields. Better to help him open doors where he can excel than force or allow him to pound on ones that will never swing out for him.

8. THE SELF-ACCEPTING CHILD ASSUMES RESPONSIBILITY FOR HIS OWN BEHAVIOR

A portion of the child's autonomy includes his capacity to think out his own problems and purposes. Every youngster should have firsthand knowledge of ways to advance his personal independence. The accepting home gives him an opportunity to play a self-reliant role within an approving base. This can help two kinds of child—the overly aggressive rule breaker, or the overly regressive timid child.

The supportive groundwork in the child's life proved vital in Oh Kyung's life. She was so young when she came to the Inchon Orphanage that she remembered nothing of how she arrived. She does say, "I cried a lot. I was afraid of my new environment and there were so many little children and the buildings seemed so big. I was a very timid little girl and even tiny problems made me cry easily. I found I was afraid to do things or even make small decisions."

At that point Oh Kyung's housemother played a key part. "She was so kind and generous with me and always fulfilled the much-needed motherly role. From her I learned what love meant. But then a few months before I graduated from high school, she suddenly died."

The housemother's death was a tremendous shock to the young girl. She felt that her whole world had tumbled in. She even entertained thoughts of suicide "in order that I might follow her to heaven—although I felt that this was a sin."

Shortly thereafter, Oh Kyung became ill with what was diagnosed as "chronic pneumonia." Her condition worsened daily and hope was abandoned for any recovery. "I was like a living skeleton and looked forward to my last day on earth."

At this point, however, a new supportive link was forged in her life—in the person of another loving housemother. "She came to see me in the hospital every day and prayed for me earnestly while she held my hands. My whole home family also prayed every day for my recovery. And at last God answered their prayers and performed a miracle. That summer my health finally began to improve and I had a new glimmer of meaning in my life."

A pattern of hesitancy became part of her life style. "I was still fearful to take initiatives even at age eighteen," she confesses. But her housemothers had nurtured and urged her into decisions that she later found led to successes.

"The spring after my recovery," she reports, "our super-intendent established a civic school [junior high level] for needy youngsters who could not afford to attend the regular junior high. She asked me if I would be willing to teach these children. I was hesitant again. But it had always been my long-cherished hope to help those who were weak and poor like me. I thought to myself, 'God has let me live just so I can help these needy girls.' "

For five years, Oh Kyung gave guidance and encouragement to these young lives, gaining more confidence and expertise daily. Later she fell in love with a seminary student, was married, and now lives in Seoul with him and her two children.

As a child is encouraged to participate, he is found to assume greater responsibility. And even the dissident child, when he is allowed to share in rule-making, is rarely involved in rule-breaking. Better yet, he will ingest the rules he himself has helped create in such a way that he will observe them whether adults are present or not.

The drive toward self-determination is inherent in every child but must be nurtured and enriched in many. The parent who shares her power with her youngster by encouraging him to become involved is allowing a responsible adult to unfold.

9. THE SELF-ACCEPTING CHILD DOES NOT CONDEMN HIMSELF FOR HAVING CERTAIN FEELINGS

Nor does he try to deny that he has these feelings. When a parent respects his child's emotions, he respects his value as a person. When feelings spring up in the child, they are evidence of his humanness. To deny them is to deny the youngster's right to be a full-fledged member of mankind.

When we say, "Temper! Temper!" to our children, we are damming up a human emotion that can be sidetracked into more destructive currents. When we step into a quarrel between two children of equal size, we are often interrupting a normal childhood problem solution.

I recall a parent attempting to settle such a quarrel between two pre-teen sisters. She picked them up from their relatively harmless struggle and brushed them off. Then she made them face one another.

"Now," she said, "I want you to kiss each other and say, 'I love you!' " The two youngsters glowered at one another and were motionless for a moment. Then the mother pushed them into each other's arms and repeated her order. Half-heartedly the children made muted kissing noises in each other's direction and mumbled, "Love ya." But their looks belied their words.

When a parent manipulates his child's emotions he is, in effect, forcing him to surrender his right to his inner self. Of course I do not advocate allowing him free rein to follow his own physical desires without control. But there is a clear distinction between *feelings* and unharnessed *acts*. His feelings are his own and need to be channeled, not stifled. "I know that you're mad, and I understand why," the parent can say, "but you'll have to take out your frustrations on something that is not alive. Go hammer on a board and show us how mad you are."

A youngster should not be made to earn love by constant good behavior. And more especially, a parent ought not to make him feel guilty for his feelings. A young child cannot be a copy of his parent's emotions and should not be expected to be. It is often hard for a parent who was raised in another generation—who was perhaps forced not only to *do* the "right" things, but to *feel* the "right" way—to be relaxed in this situation.

10. THE SELF-ACCEPTING CHILD BELIEVES GOD LOVES AND ACCEPTS HIM

This makes it easier for him to accept himself. He knows his weaknesses and which faults he can change. If he knows that he has a hair-trigger temper, he can learn to route it through harmless bypasses. But better than that, he knows that God loves him "no matter what."

It is especially hard for an orphan to feel this acceptance, when society often literally does reject him. Marong felt this particularly in Indonesia. "Both my parents died when I was very little. I remember crying as I followed their coffins to the graveyard after a terrible epidemic." Shortly thereafter the boy was admitted to a Christian orphanage where he found the warm acceptance of other children.

"But," he says, "when I went into the world, it was different. To become a member of society is not easy for an orphan whom people do not trust. Their cold eyes made me feel lonely many times, and life was a continuous challenge.

"When I eventually went out to work at sixteen, I worked very diligently, having to sleep on the chairs at night—for I had no place else. One day they accused me falsely of stealing and I was dismissed. I was bitter and angry, but tried to console myself by reading poetry. It did not help much. I became so desperate that I finally turned back to the orphanage to see if they could help.

"There again I found the constant love of God whom I had forgotten for a while. His love was very warm and tender. I remember how much the sponsors and Christian training had meant to me as a lonely child, and rededicated my heart to Jesus. I had to work and study hard to find a place in society, but with God's help I have done so."

Paul Tournier makes the remark, "Once the kind of life that depends on grace has been glimpsed, it is never forgotten." He tells of a young woman whose married life had immersed her in many overwhelming problems. She then recalled a short stay she had had ten years previously in a Christian retreat where the members had been vitally filled with faith. In the middle of all her difficulties she suddenly had the feeling that dark clouds would part and let light shine through.

Dr. Dan Poling used to tell of an experience from his childhood. As children he and a friend put together a raft and floated down a rushing river. The experience soon turned from fun to excitement and then to fear. Other playmates alerted his family to Dan's danger, and they raced parallel to the river to a spot where they thought the raft might land.

He recalled being pulled wet and shaking from the river by his father. "I still recall the feel of my father's arms around me. His voice was a mixture of concern and love. 'My son,' he groaned, 'my son.'

"It must be a reflection of just such love at the infinite level that the Father has for each of his children," said Poling.

Dr. James Angel has written a beautiful prayer that illustrates our eternal return to the Father:

Heavenly Parent:
We give up. We aren't going to try anymore to understand your love for your children. You made a perfect world. You looked it over. You said it looked good to you. You gave it to us, and we broke it . . .

You kept on loving the world, flawed and faulted. You loved the world so much that you sent a Son to live and die and live again for all the people on the earth. We don't understand. We give up. It's too much for our minds . . .

One of your Son's young men grew old and saw visions. He saw a world where people would hunger no more, or thirst either. He said you would wipe away every tear from people's lives. We like that. We do some crying ourselves. Our mission will be to feed people and to satisfy thirst. We will dry a few tears . . .

You gave us choices, but you don't make it easy. We are haunted by the voice of Jesus of Galilee. The Holy Spirit permits no hiding place. You invite us to a mission of good news . . .

We sign up for mission for keeps. We will not understand your love, but we will not quit your mission . . .

In the foregoing pages we have talked about the way a child can learn to accept himself in the light of the Father's love. But there are those moments when a child steps out of a parent's guidelines—still loved—but erring. The next chapter will attempt to indicate how a youngster can be brought back "into orbit" through sensitive discipling.

FIVE
DISCIPLINING HIM
THROUGH DISCIPLESHIP

Webster describes discipline as "a course of training which corrects, molds, strengthens or perfects," a primary definition. Unfortunately, secondary definitions such as "punishment," "chastisement," and "penalty" often pop into our minds when the word is mentioned. This is sad. When Jesus said, "You shall be my disciples," he had something else in mind. The early disciples followed him out of deep persuasion. They did not feel punished into being his disciples.

True discipline grows out of love, causing St. Augustine to say, "Love God and do as you please." He knew that the soul who deeply loves the Father does nothing to displease him.

Ideally punishment should never be necessary. But we all live in that real world where there comes "the moment of truth," when we must punish our child. But we do have some choices. We *can* punish in anger. Or we *may* do it because it is a great catharsis for our irritation. Or it is possible we may be "getting even" with our father who punished us for this same misdeed years before. But hopefully our punishment will grow out of a profound love for the child and desire for his proper growth. In such instances our punishment can bear fruit.

Tournier has said, "You give a child advice. Your state of mind is far more important than the advice itself. You may be inspired by fear . . . and in this case you will inspire fear in him. But if you are inspired by prudent and trusting wisdom, this same advice will be useful."

Much misbehavior stems from a child's need to be loved and to feel secure. As a result, he feels hurt, angry, or frightened. The parent needs to give the youngster a normal amount of affection and security. And the child needs to be assured that he is loved in spite of his misbehavior. Further, the father or mother needs to discover what it was that hurt, angered, or frightened the child. In the end, the adult may still feel that the child needs punishment. But such punishment can now be given on the basis of understanding the child and with the child's cooperation. The child should grow as a person with the help of good discipline. But discipline should have certain characteristics.

1. DISCIPLINE SHOULD BE THE NATURAL RESULT OF THE MISBEHAVIOR

For example, a boy who has broken a window in anger should be required to help repair the damage. The ultimate goal here, of course, is self-regulation. And this in turn depends on a strong self-image as a responsible person. Each misdeed requires individualized attention, since no two children are the same. Despite the fact that two children grow up in the same family, each has a different environment. One has an older sibling; the other does not. Every parent needs to study each of his children. One is an extrovert, one an ambivert, and still another an introvert. Natural discipline should flow not only from the situation, but from the personality of the child himself.

Kim Yong was a skilled little carpenter with a "short fuse," and as a result his classmates delighted in teasing him. One day he was pushed too far and in his anger broke a small table in the classroom while scuffling with another lad. The other boy was required to clean up the mess they had both made. Kim Yong was required to repair the broken leg on the table. It allowed him to utilize his carpentry skill and thereby grow, while such punishment was a natural result of the misdeed. It was a small step on the journey toward personal responsibility.

One mother had constant difficulty getting her child to eat his meal. He would linger over his food and talk to himself. Finally the mother was advised simply to remove the meal from him after a reasonable time. Eventually after she had done this several times, the boy found himself complaining about hunger halfway through the morning. "I'm sorry, dear," she would remind him, "but you should have eaten your breakfast when I gave it to you." An empty stomach is a natural outgrowth of dawdling over breakfast. Scolding or punishment does not produce results quite so quickly as a growling stomach.

2. DISCIPLINE SHOULD BE CONSISTENT

If a parent laughs at a certain misdeed at one time and punishes it the next, the child can become totally confused.

I have seen one mother, very relaxed on certain days, allow her children to "get away with murder." But in moments of tension, she clamps down on them with anger and punishment for identical deeds. Bewilderment follows—and often, defiance.

Another problem that occurs leading to inconsistency is a difference in discipline style between father and mother. The mother may tend to be stricter than her mate, and the child quickly learns to play off one against the other.

I overheard one child say to her brother,

"If you want to go on a bike ride Saturday, ask Dad. Don't ask Mom. She'll say no on general principles!"

Parents need to agree on basic ground rules so that children will not play this round-robin with discipline.

3. DISCIPLINE SHOULD BE FAIR

As in law, so in child care, "the punishment should fit the crime." Too often a parent may make a federal case out of a minor misdeed and have no ammunition left for really major ones.

Further, to deprive a child of something essential to his growth can not only be unfair but damaging to his health and welfare. To withhold meals, to isolate him in a cold room in the winter, to subject him to ridicule or embarrassment—all of these and similar punishments can do lasting harm. Not only can they be a hazard, but they can also create anger and bitterness that may last into adulthood.

Which of us does not still simmer from real or imagined injustices in discipline when we were children. One lad who was dismissed from a class for a misdeed he did not perform, still bristles to this day at the memory of the unfairness. Although forty years have now passed, he can still relive the scene, the humiliation, and the anger. The teacher who did it to him is long departed, but bitterness remains.

One lad was accused of stealing money from his mother's purse, and was not guilty. The severe discipline left a lasting mark. More particularly, he was not allowed to plead his cause and prove his innocence.

Another youngster in one of the orphanages was punished for eating some fruit he was harvesting. Perhaps the superintendent might have asked the children to work hard, and they would have a recess for fruit-eating at a proper moment. Arbitrary and harsh punishment without recourse is as unfair for children as it would be for adults.

Granted, at times it takes good judgment and a level head to make disciplinary decisions. It is the price of responsible parenthood.

Of course, fairness works both ways. If the child has genuinely misbehaved, his maturity will only grow by facing the consequences. Dr. James Dobson in his fine book, *Dare to Discipline*, comments on the father in the Lord's parable.

"First," he says, "the father did not try to locate the son and drag him home. The boy was apparently old enough to make his own decision, and his father allowed him the privilege."

Too often, we intervene with advice or force, when *experience* must do the teaching.

"Second," continues Dr. Dobson, "the father did not come to his rescue during the financial stress that followed."

A child that breaks his own bike should fix it. A boy or girl dismissed from school should experience the aftermath. Sometimes, sadly, life itself can deal unjust results to a

youngster. As John Kennedy once said, "Life *can* be unfair!"
A child needs to learn even this occasionally.

4. GOOD PUNISHMENT SHOULD BALANCE THE MATTER OF ANGER AND IMPERSONALITY

There are two reliable schools of thought about this. "Should
I ever punish a child when I am angry?" Dr. Fitzhugh Dodson
(in *How to Parent*) contends, "Never strike a child *except* in
anger!" This runs counter to many psychologists, but
deserves some consideration. "A child can understand very
well when you strike him in anger." First, because he "digs"
anger himself, and has experienced it many times in his short
lifetime. Under most circumstances he knows quite well
why the parent is angry.

I clearly recall a spanking I administered to my youngest
daughter when she was three. It was governed, I must confess,
out of fear and anger. We had moved into a new neighborhood
and she had disappeared for three hours. My wife and I looked
frantically for her, called neighbors that we knew, and did
a lot of praying. Finally she wandered home, singing to herself
with her doll in tow. She had been visiting an elderly neighbor
down the block.

Both Mary and I recall the incident vividly. "You spanked
me right over the furnace register," she reminisces. "I knew
why you punished me. You were frightened for my safety. I
forgave you long ago."

The anger and the ugly are realities of life. Bruno Bettelheim
has written an enlightening book, *The Meaning of Enchant-
ment*. In it he contends that fairy tales—even scary ones—are
vital for child rearing. They enable the youngster to
think through the frightfulness of life and of parents at an
imaginary level. He argues that the world is filled with adult
ogres and giants with which the child must contend. It is
part of the puzzle of life, and important that he grapple with
it at a mythical level. Dream and reality are not too far apart
in solving life's riddle.

There is another view, however, on punishing in anger. The
parent should as much as possible avoid punishing a child

when he is really angry about something else. Even then, however, a child can understand when the parent says, "Jack, I'm sorry. You did a wrong thing, but I lost my temper. I was worried about the money I lost yesterday." Admitting anger to the youngster is important for your relationship with him, and helps him deal with the problem of temper.

As in psychiatric counseling, most methods of interpersonal problem-settling will work—as long as love is present! The child has a sixth sense that tells him when we are dealing out of love—or from some other less worthy motive.

Dr. Dubois of Berne, Switzerland, was one of the pioneers of modern psychotherapy. He knew this truth in the early part of the twentieth century. "Hold out your hand to that person," he said. "Do not be afraid of frankly admitting to him your weaknesses, your inborn shortcomings. Bring yourself close to him." The key to punishment, whether in anger or unemotionalism, is that the parent have a deep concern.

A Christian psychiatrist once said to me, "Freudian counseling will work for you, and so will Rogerian counseling. But one common requisite is essential—that you *care!*"

5. GOOD DISCIPLINE SHOULD LEAD THE CHILD TO BETTER SELF-CONTROL

Here is an opportunity for the child to contribute to his own form of punishment. "How do you feel you should be punished?" he might be asked. "How would you carry it out?" After all, good discipline teaches the child to govern himself.

Many parents unfortunately have little confidence in the child's ability to do things for himself. A good motto might be, "Never do anything for your child that he himself can perform." This applies to good discipline as well as other matters.

Sooner or later, the moment of discipline will arrive for every child. There is no such thing as a *model* youngster. A so-called model child is neither genuine nor self-governing. He is displaying a false front. We need to get through to the genuine article beneath such a veneer. A young person who always keeps the Scout law—is *always* trustworthy, loyal, helpful, courteous, etc.—is not acting like a real child. He is a child masquerading as an adult.

One of Dr. Tournier's patients once said to him, "All my reactions are those of a child but I have to hide them behind a personage which acts and speaks like a grownup!" If this is true of some adults, how much more so of the normal child.

From one of our homes in Hong Kong comes the story of the mischievous boys who were gaily celebrating the completion of their examinations. The boys roamed a back alley in the Kowloon area in the late afternoon, overturning garbage receptacles or "dustbins," causing real havoc. Finally collared by the police, they were brought wriggling to their houseparent. Would the home punish the youngsters, or should the police?

"The best discipline I can conceive," said Mr. Hong, their housefather, "is for the boys to retrace their steps and replace every piece of garbage to the dustbins!"

He told them: "I want you to divide up the street and each take responsibility for one section. And I want it to look neater now than it did before you did the damage."

It was an unsavory task, but it initiated a sense of civic pride in the boys. There developed a competitive spirit between them to see which section of the street would appear the neatest.

The best use of self-control is in interpersonal responsibility. Here is the hardest situation in which to discipline—when one child has wronged another. Jacques Ellul of the Protestant Congress in France has defined it: "To be responsible is to have to reply." The two great questions that God first asked man were: "Where are you, Adam?" and (to Cain) "Where is your brother?" In brief, "What have you done to your brother—and what has happened to the bond that united you?"

Restitution between brother and brother, when one has wronged the other, is the most difficult discipline to administer. But the solution worked out between them personally should be the sweetest form of human relationships, a healing experience above all others. My own fights with my brother a half-century ago still stand out in my memory—not so much because of the quarrels but because of the truces that led me to understand him more deeply.

6. GOOD DISCIPLINE WITHHOLDS PUNISHMENT UNTIL THE PARENT KNOWS ALL THE FACTS

"Why did the child do the deed?" "What provoked him?" "What frightened him?" "What upset his security?" "What thoughtless childhood act led him astray?" "What hostility?" It is possible that when the mother discovers the answers, she may have little to punish.

In Tijuana recently, a six-year-old child, José Rodriguez, was accidentally burned. Later the mother explored the reasons for the accident. One child had played with matches. Other children had toyed with gasoline. The playmate lit a match at exactly the moment gasoline was spilled. José's mother had been marketing and neighbors had to piece together the sad episode for her. The child was dreadfully scarred, but in his severest pain he could not cry. "I was afraid my daddy would beat me," he said.

Consider the teacher who turns her back on the class for a moment and discovers a misdeed. She may be quick to judge. "OK, Jerry," she says, "stay after school for an hour." In point of fact, it was not Jerry who had played the prank. Despite his protestations, she must maintain her "discipline." Jerry is her scapegoat this year.

Unfairness can leave lasting scars. One child is told repeatedly when she stammers, "You've got rocks in your head!" She has speech problems but is quite intelligent. Nevertheless the parent does not probe into the youngster's emotional difficulty. It is easier to believe her brainless. The child will grow up inwardly crippled.

When a child is called stupid, he can become stupid, unable to demonstrate what is really in him. A beautiful little girl may be told by her mother that she is ugly. Such a person can become so devoid of confidence that when someone later openly admires her, she interprets it as disdain.

7. GOOD DISCIPLINE AVOIDS AROUSING FEAR

Particularly the disturbed or neurotic child has already known far too much fear. More of it only further disorganizes him. Dr. Sears in his *Patterns of Child-Rearing* says, "Our evaluation of severity is that it is ineffectual in the long term as a technique for eliminating the kind of behavior toward which it is directed." If we are overbearing enough, we can destroy our child's mettle. Tyranny is perfect for a youngster who is going to live in a despotic land. But it can never help a child who is destined for democracy.

Fear under an authoritarian parent results in a child's damaged self-image. It teaches him that he cannot rely on his own abilities in judgment or insight.

Severity will fail for a variety of reasons. Most important—it relies entirely on power—parent-power. And such power is usually employed for the benefit of the parent, not the child.

"Let's restore the whip!" some of the media appeal, as they search for methods of crime prevention. However, studies at Harvard indicate that between 60 and 90 percent of delinquents in prison had been administered severe physical punishment before their arrest. Only 30 percent of non-delinquent boys received such handling.

Dr. Hugh Missildine tells of a boy who was thrown into a reformatory for retaliating against a brutal environment. For cursing he was made to hold a piece of soap in his mouth for several hours. For trying to run away he was put into a freezing room with only a thin nightshirt to wear. For stealing a few apples he was brutally beaten. Mistreatment after mistreatment piled up until in his own words he concluded:

"I was treated like a beast and I began to act like a beast . . .
I have come and gone from one institution to another. I am only twenty, but I have gone through five different places and am about to go through my sixth . . . ."

In brief, many of our severest punishments do not teach. Sometimes a parent will conclude that a child is beyond hope, but it is often his own severity that has confirmed the child in "badness." Eventually vindictive retaliation becomes embedded in the youngster.

However, it need be said that authoritarianism *occasionally* applied will not do irreparable harm. Studies have shown that a firm pat on the posterior actually can reinforce the message and add to a child's sense of security provided it is administered in love. It is only when dictatorship in the home strikes an all-pervasive note that the child's future is threatened. A frightened or threatened child will usually agree to anything for the time being. But after he has recovered it is likely that his behavior will be worse than before.

8. GUIDING LOVE MUST REIGN

Much misbehavior on the part of a child comes from a need to be loved, to feel secure, or to be guided. If he is manifestly striking back, the parents will want to look beneath the surface for a hurt, an anger, a fright, or a bewilderment. Many children are asking for a firm hand with the spoken or unspoken cry, "Dad should *make* me mind!"

The loving parent can shore up his child with a normal degree of kindness and security. The youngster needs confirmation that he is loved despite his misdeed. At the same time the parent will want to probe for that fright, anger, or hurt. Discipline can then be administered on the basis of understanding and cooperation. The youngster needs to continue to grow as a person, and good discipline is one of the paths.

However, it is anything but an easy road. It takes tremendous forbearance. It enjoins a disposition for hard and cooperative effort. Every child has those "impossible" moments. He will sometimes kick or scream and make the parent "anxious." And the parent's worry will communicate itself to the child. Rigidity and anxiety will have its lasting effect. A parent needs to relax as much as he can and take upsets in stride, as a normal phenomenon of growth.

One of the sad stories from the literary world is that of Sylvia Plath, a young woman endowed with tremendous talent but forever on the edge of psychosis.

It began when Sylvia was eight and her deeply loved father died. After the mother had given her the news, Sylvia's comment was, "I am never going to talk to God again!" When the message of death had penetrated sufficiently she made her mother promise with a signed oath, "I promise I will never marry again."

Thereafter she lived her life with a dreadful intensity, and her mother allowed herself to be swallowed up in Sylvia's identity. Aurelia Plath was ever after a devoted servant to her daughter's singular drives.

According to *Time* magazine (Nov. 24, 1975), Sylvia was capable of an emotional fixity that makes her poems almost unbearable to read, particularly those written just before her suicide in 1963. Her book *The Bell Jar* apparently satirizes her mother as a narrow-minded, hardworking WASP parent.

Yet there was a symbiosis between mother and child that both recognized, different as they were in temperament. It is the sort of relationship that must be avoided if both parent and child are to live normal lives. Before her first suicide attempt, Sylvia clasped her mother's hand and said, "Oh Mother, the world is so rotten! I want to die! Let's die together!"

Time's comment at the close of its article on her life is a telling one: "It is now clear that the end came for Sylvia [after her second suicide attempt] not only because she lost her own husband, but because she could no longer grasp her mother's hand."

As the child matures, it is the privilege of each Christian parent to transfer that young hand over to a greater One—one lacking in Sylvia's life. There is no greater verse in the spiritual life of the child than Isaiah's:

"I am holding you by your right hand—I the Lord your God —and I say to you, Don't be afraid; I am here to help you" (41:13).

9. SOME HEALTHY OUTLETS AS PREVENTIVES OF MISBEHAVIOR

The parent can be constantly exploring for methods whereby the child may find healthy outlets for emotions. By providing opportunities for expressing such perturbations a practical catharsis is provided for emotions as they are aroused. Among these methods are: interest groups, organized games, interesting jobs, development of appropriate skills and, above all, a personal and spiritual fellowship as provided in church and youth groups:

Formation of committees with interesting projects. As I have spoken to groups of young people through the Western world, I have found an eager response to needs of hungry children. There are now many agencies providing opportunity to sponsor a disinherited child on the other side of the globe in a third-world nation. Youth groups, YMCAs, fraternities, Scout troops, Cubs, and Brownies are just a few of the organizations that have volunteered with enthusiasm to assume care for a hungry boy or girl in India, Latin America, or Africa. For a few dollars a month they enter into the life of a needy waif, receive a photo, write to him or her, and vicariously feed, clothe, educate the child.

From one such group came this letter recently:

We have tacked Andhra's story and picture on our class bulletin board so that we can look at her dark eyes. Her case history tells us that she is lame, but it says perhaps someday her leg can be straightened. We hope so. We are having a car wash this Saturday to start saving money for an operation. Some of our girls have volunteered to baby-sit and give money to the operation fund. Several boys are doing odd jobs in people's yards to earn money for the cause.

We have just received our first letter from Andhra. She sounds so cheerful after what she has been through. We are praying for her now regularly. We have so much and she has so little. Enclosed is an extra five dollars. Would you please see that she gets a pretty new dress from the local market there in her little town. God bless you. We all send our love to her.

The children's enthusiasm and hard work have left little time for negative emotions.

The formation of discussion groups, too, either formal or informal, makes room for a creativity that can have lasting value. "Man is a talkative creature," and the youngsters find great emotional satisfaction in expressing themselves in words.

The organizing of games of all sorts gives top priority for a child to work off pent-up hostilities and is a device as ancient as man himself. Moreover, it is an opportunity for a child to discover more concerning his core person. Each child's body constantly relays to him new messages about himself. Charles, for example, has a well-articulated and muscular body. He is one of the gifted to whom sports come easily. Other youngsters compete for his attention and the privilege of being on his team. His ability gives him a certain aplomb and mirrors to him an ability for self-control—a valuable lesson when he is tempted to misbehave. He has learned to like himself too well to employ pettiness.

Here also is a built-in diversion from striking out blindly at a hostile world. It allows Charles the opportunity to kick or bat a ball with vigor instead of hitting another child or pet. Physical exertion uses up excess blood sugar with which his muscles are already provided and allows them to relax again. And games are especially good for Charles as compensation, since he does not do too well in math and language.

Undoubtedly one of the most important lessons for any child is that of *honesty* learned in games. Karl Menninger in his *Vital Balance* has said, "One can bluff, one can lie, one can pretend all sorts of things just as long as he does not take for himself an advantage which the others have foresworn with him. One instance of 'cheating' and he is out of the game permanently. 'Play' which reverts to undisguised aggression is unacceptable."

Any kind of extra work, occupation, or skill may also function therapeutically, lessening misbehavior and heightening character growth. By such creativity many a child has found himself. The home in Nazareth imparted this lesson through the hands of Joseph and the boy Jesus as carpentry was taught and learned. It is exciting to watch an awakening enthusiasm in a child's eyes. He is learning not only to do something well but to benefit others.

Dr. Frank Barron has done considerable research on the subject of creativity and makes a distinction between two kinds. There is the creativity that seeps from a *repressed* unconscious and is the counterfeit variety. And then there is the genuine form that will flow without inhibition from an unchained unconscious.

Joni Eareckson, the quadriplegic heroine whose life was

devastated by a diving accident, is a perfect illustration of the latter—genuine creativity flowing from open-handed love. Joni has appeared on American television illustrating how she learned to paint beautiful landscapes with a brush in her teeth, since she is paralyzed from the shoulders down. It is a perfect compensation for what seems to be a hopeless case. Joni's ringing testimony and her dependence on God are evident in every word.

Joni's recovery contrasts painfully with Sylvia Plath's defeat as two ways that young people may react to their environment and circumstances. Probably one secret is found in the two young women's disparate family settings. A loving, nurturing home life cocooned Joni through the staggering onslaughts. Sylvia's home, on the other hand, may have lacked many of these essentials. In the next chapter we will endeavor to examine family patterns that can "make or break" the child.

SIX
FORMING HIS IDEAL FAMILY

Koo Wan's last words were, "Bring up one of my sons as a pastor." It was part of a story common to the early fifties when Korea was rocked by attack and counterattack. "Many persons were sacrificed at that time," Mrs. Kim writes, "but we were able to make many friends. At that time as we were crossing a turbulent river one afternoon, I met a famous but ailing evangelist named Koo Wan. He and his six little children were tied together around the waist so that they would not be swept away with the current."

Mrs. Kim joined them at the far edge of the torrent with children she was rescuing from her bombed-out orphanage. As they trudged southward, shells and planes threatened them constantly. Pastor Koo Wan grew rapidly weaker as they journeyed during the next few weeks. When they finally arrived at an empty house in Sun San, they found that he was in terminal stages of stomach cancer. As he lay on a floor pallet, his six youngsters clustered around him, along with Mrs. Kim, to bid goodbye. His final words made a lasting impression on Jang Hae, the oldest, who was twelve. With tears, he promised his dying father he would work hard, take care of his brothers and sisters and, in the end, become a minister.

Jang persevered through middle school and finished high school with honors. Eventually he made it through college and seminary. "It was due to his enduring nature," Mrs. Kim remarked. But probably just as important was the affectionate relationship between Jang and his father during formative years. Recent research at Purdue has indicated that "the warm responsiveness a parent provides for the child forms the primary foundation for a future positive view of self."

The continual communication between Jang Hae and his parent established a steady flow of spiritual undergirding. After the father's death, as someone has graphically put it, "the tape kept right on running!"

A deeper look at such family relationships warrants more than casual analysis.

In studying, for example, the Smith family's life style and pattern for interaction, it is usually clearer to a casual stranger than to one of the household members. An observer will perceive characteristics in this family that are peculiar to itself. He notices the degree of affection and can see that the home is notably relaxed. If he were a trained visitor, he could probably categorize the Smiths in one of three rubrics determined by the behavior of Mr. and Mrs. Smith:

1. A family sociologist would observe the *degree* of acceptance which the Smiths display toward their children. He would note whether they accept each youngster far more than they reject. It would be obvious whether they are casual or indifferent to their little ones.

2. In visiting for a moment with the Gregorys, another typical home, we find a second pivotal aspect of family constellations. It is the *dimension of indulgence* that one feels might exceed the norm. For instance, Johnny Gregory seems to get everything his heart desires. Mary, the only daughter, has her own car long before other children in the neighborhood do. The extent to which parents indulge children, or deny them entirely, has a strong bearing on later adult "passages."

3. A third and deciding factor is *the authority-pattern* in the family. For example, the Andersons have structured an autocratic hierarchy and each child jumps to Mr. Anderson's command. On the other hand, the MacDuffys seem to have developed a democratic household that allows for each child's appropriate contribution.

It is from these basic attitudes that sociologists have derived *at least eight rather common patterns of family living*. Most homes will likely find themselves in a synthesis of two or more of these narrowly defined categories. Much depends on heritage, emotional pressures, and stress at each adult phase, but particularly important is how one's own parents have designed his childhood.

The first of the patterns is the *actively rejecting family*, illustrated by the Cross family. The Crosses are basically "losers" in the battle of life. As I have observed them, they are a hostile couple with no apparent love for their children. If so, it is well hidden. I have watched an unloving and critical handling of their two boys and one girl. There appears to be a continual distancing of the children from their primary concerns. The love of God and church is certainly not in evidence.

The moments of child-parent contact I have seen have been mainly those of crisp commands. "Joan, for the third time, take out the garbage!" "Jake, cut out that G-D racket!" I have never seen evidence of a warm, social, or trusting relationship. Instead, anger rules.

Mrs. Cross clearly resents having children, and her children repay her resentment with compound interest. It is clear that both she and her husband really dislike children in general and their own in particular. Their high school education has given them no insight into even basic elements of child psychology, and they prefer not to hear about them. Hostile nagging is the elemental form of dialogue.

The Crosses operate on a cold, unsympathetic level with symptoms of irritability toward each child when he is around. "The kids are a nuisance," they tell me.

The second family pattern can be observed in the Johnson's home. It has been termed the *indifferent-rejecting* family. The Johnsons are similar to the Crosses in that they have a basic dislike for children; but they lack the "nit-picking" approach. As I have watched Grace Johnson I have noted indifference as a major emotion regarding her two youngsters. She and her husband, George, ignore them as completely as possible. Contacts with them are kept to a minimum. The only times of excitement or anger are displayed when the children accidentally get in their way.

At such crisis moments the Johnsons quickly resort to authoritarian techniques. I do not detect any malice toward the youngsters, simply expediency. They clearly wish to settle a problem as quickly as possible and move on to more interesting matters.

The Atkins family represents *the third* of these patterns—*the casually autocratic home.* I have met this kind of parent in varying circumstances and find him more dictatorial than others. He seems to stand midway in the spectrum of parental syndromes—neither accepting his four children with understanding nor rejecting them with resentment. As I have talked to Mr. Atkins, it is clear that he never doubts the superiority of his own viewpoint and authority over that of his children's. Should there ever be a choice between a child's wishes and his own, he wins hands-down.

The fourth pattern is probably very typical of Western families—*the casually indulgent home.* The Hotchkiss household typifies this one as well as any. They have two youngsters, Bonnie and David, and are quite benign toward the children's wishes. They allow the two, in their early teens, to come and go in a most undemanding fashion. The home itself is haphazard, but the climate is pleasant to visit, and I am sure the children find it agreeable. There are few big arguments about what David or Bonnie can do—the children apparently have *carte blanche* for most of their whims. I have never seen either parent excessively indulgent, but as Mrs. Hotchkiss put it to me one day, "In the long run, it's easier to say yes than no!"

The Hotchkisses accept their children in a relaxed manner. Even though twelve-year-old David had been away on a week-long camping trip, I saw him received home with little fanfare—a simple pat seemed to suffice. The children accept this offhand way of living and apparently expect little else.

In contrast to many sterner households, I have never heard the Hotchkisses lay down a firm law that required strict obedience. I did see them once have a brief confrontation over some apparent infraction, but it was shortlived. The children maneuvered their parents to another subject easily.

One final interesting note, the Hotchkisses from time to time seem to "baby" their youngsters more than the norm. Assumption of societal responsibilities may be somewhat difficult for David and Bonnie in future years, although not so difficult as for a child in the *fifth family pattern*.

Dr. Missildine (in *Your Inner Child of the Past*) has pointed out symptoms of overindulgence when a child reaches adulthood. "If you are generally bored, unable to become interested enough in activities to participate in them, find yourself not wanting to do what others find satisfying . . . your life is being dominated by an overly indulged 'inner child of the past.' "

The Leacocks' home would probably be termed the *accepting-indulgent family*, the fifth in these categories. Jack and Amanda Leacock are a middle-class couple in New Jersey who are deeply and emotionally attached to their two youngsters, Mike and James. They tend to be unusually anxious about the boys' welfare. Friends often advise them, "Stop trying to live your youngsters' lives for them." But to no avail. They not only live for them, but attempt to experience their lives *through* them.

While the Hotchkisses baby their two mildly, the Leacocks clearly *over*protect and mollycoddle James and Mike. Mrs. Leacock is the prototype for whom the term "smother-love" was created. She goes to endless lengths to satisfy her boys' whims. Every afternoon she picks them up at school and drives them to some new assignment—piano, dancing, tennis, parties. On Saturdays Mr. Leacock hovers above their little league baseball and football or other sports function—an extreme of the sideline umpire or referee, making a fuss over their slightest injuries. Weekends are totally devoted to the children.

Yet, with all the indulgence, Amanda and Jack do not admit the children as equals to decision-making functions of the family. Their care for the boys appears neurotic and guilt-ridden. They brood endlessly over omissions in their nurturing function.

"I just can't help it," Amanda told me, "I worry about them constantly. I can't think of them as other children. I need to watch them in the smallest detail." This lack of objectivity has a definite bearing on standards they set for their children's behavior. They can never relax as do the Hotchkisses; in fact, they look on such neighbors with horror. Rules are clearly delineated, although not necessarily written down. James and Mike know the dos and don'ts by heart and argue endlessly between themselves as to the rightness or wrongness of certain ventures. Even the nuances of behavior are examined in detail.

"I asked Mom," Mike told James, "if we could go to Disneyland and she said, 'We'll see.' That means yes."

"Not always," said James. "Sometimes I have known 'We'll see' to mean no."

Many of us as parents find ourselves echoing the Leacocks' thoughts and ask ourselves, "Where did I get this pattern?"

Dr. Roger Gould in his book *Transformations* says,

"Every time we respond to our child or make a decision about him, we conform to or deny our own parents. This surviving unconscious memory of our own childhood is the basis for our empathy with or understanding of our child. It is a marvelously designed system for automatically reproducing the next generation as a replica of the former generation."

Yet in our normal human reaction, we reply, "But things are rather different today. Circumstances have changed. I want my child to be able to adapt to this wildly fluctuating culture."

This leads Dr. Gould to add, "This all worked very well when cultural change was slow, but it's not so good in this era of rapid cultural flux. We want our children to be free of our bad characteristics."

It was divinely planned that our Lord enter history bringing a gospel for just such adaptation. We hear him saying, "You have heard how it was said of old, 'Thou shalt' . . . but I say unto you . . . I came not to destroy the law but to fulfill . . . My purpose is to give life in all its fullness."

This fullness of life is the excitement we can impart to our children's experience within a firm structure of Christian ethics. Paul Tournier describes it as a "need for fulfillment that is part of the stuff of life itself. It is a need for personal adventure which is peculiar to man, a thirst for the absolute, which in the last analysis is an expression of man's hunger and thirst for God."

Don Karas, a New York publisher who has earned millions, strives for simplicity of life for his children's sake. He worries about the effect that wealth can have on youngsters in this age. "Kids can too easily get the notion," he says, "that they are the 'haves' and don't have to struggle any more. I want to make my children achievement-oriented." One way that he does this is to have his twin boys pay for their own sports equipment out of money they earn doing chores.

This probably best describes the Anderson family of Michigan. Sociologists might term them an *accepting-casual-indulging home*. Although they have their indulgent moments, they do not follow the extremes of the Leacocks. They give fairly generous allowances, as does Mr. Karas, but they expect the children to live within those limits. Otherwise, any indulgences they give the children, Karen and Alice, are given on impulse, often for a holiday, or on returning from a long absence. The Andersons do not seem to identify themselves neurotically with their youngsters, nor do they brood over any shortcomings as parents.

They are not a perfect family and sometimes allow Karen and Alice what some might call "unwarranted freedom." In fact, church friends occasionally complain of Alice's disobedience in Sunday school and Karen's occasional bad manners. Charles and Betty Anderson admit these short-comings in their children somewhat ruefully, but explain it thus:

"We prefer the children have a bit of freedom so that they can develop their gifts. We don't like to make a federal case out of everything but want to save our punishments for real transgressions."

One clear advantage that the Andersons seem to have over the Leacocks is an absence of "smother-love." They do not appear to need to be overly protective. While they want the child to follow basic Christian ethics, they do not niggle over each detail of living as do the Leacocks. Nor do they feel guilty over this omission.

One of the elements of grace is freedom of choice. Nancy Mayer, an authority in the field of mental health, has put her finger on this: "Sometimes the father over-identifies with his child, even his youngster's potency in defying authority. This usually leads to resignation with almost complete abdication of the fathering role. Or else he resorts to a kind of detached hand-wringing and nagging with no effective limit-setting. Instead of a conflict over content, the parent should recognize the adolescent's *right to choose*."

There is a delicate balance here—when to let go and when to limit the child. Only the well-adjusted, Spirit-led parent knows for sure. And what parent is that well-balanced all the time? Parents and children need to learn to forgive and understand a lot.

In this age of freedom (and often "license"), homes may resort to the family design of the Greggs. They are basically indulgent with their three—Joe, Anna, and Marie. They clearly believe in treating youngsters as equals in their family democracy. They encourage their children to be mildly critical of their own parental behavior and to be quite outspoken from their child-viewpoint.

They hold regular family tribunals in which the children get an equal vote on most minor issues in the household and even on some major ones.

On vacations: "Let's go to Oregon—we have had enough of the Sierras!"

On expenditures: "Let's get rid of our old car and get a new one!"

On attitudes: "Mom and Dad, you are so square!"
Family decisions do not always follow children's views, but will often be colored by them.

On the surface, the children are treated as though they are adults. But as one penetrates appearances, it becomes clear that the children are subject to a great deal of firm but gentle parental pressure. This is applied indirectly through a close bond of love between the Greggs and their children. They use "democratic" methods as a means of making their children into good companions and Christian citizens.

The Greggs' home is an interesting one to visit since it is so obviously child-centered. Furniture and entertainment are

geared to the young people's level. Family plans revolve around
the children's schedule. The household agenda seems to
depend on a mildly neurotic degree of contact between parent
and child.

Probably the Greggs reflect the home in Nazareth as well as
most, recalling at a deeper level the eternal gospel as an
extension of the family of God. It might help us to examine this
pattern a bit more in depth with its undertone of Christian
value.

Dan and Maureen Gregg have worked out a complex but
unified system of household authority based on their common
love for God. This life-view has become so much a part of
their thinking that one partner knows without asking what the
other's reaction will be in a given situation. Hence their
home life has become a joint activity. In some areas Dan will
accede to Maureen in decision making because he feels that
particular concern is outside his field. Similarly Maureen backs
away when a determination must be made in Dan's field of
expertise. The couple has become quite flexible in adjustments
to each other and to circumstances.

Both parents have developed a friendly method to avoid
fights or differences of opinion. Even in the event of sharp
quarrels they are soon settled. After twelve years of marriage
they have learned ways of avoiding conflict, especially when
they know that the other partner is upset, tired, or irritable.
By now, too, they know how to withdraw a point when
struggling for it doesn't seem worthwhile.

My visits in the Greggs' home have proven to me that they
both possess an abundant supply of humor. I have watched
them repeatedly kid one another out of an overly serious
confrontation.

Dr. Carl Morgan, dean of Eastern Baptist Theological
Seminary, used to tell his students, "If I were to rewrite the
wedding ceremony, I would tell the young couple, 'And finally,
dear friends, thou shalt have a sense of humor!' "

GOOD TRAITS OF A CHRISTIAN HOME

As we conclude this overview of family life, both weaknesses
and strengths, we probably need to examine once more what

might be considered the *good traits of a Christian home.* There
are four of them, and they deal mainly with good relationships
rather than economic status:

1. The first trait of a good home is founded on the fact that
it will gradually release control of the children. Such slow
release starts even in babyhood.

The Schultz family, parented by Gerald and Jenny, has
started preparing for the children's family quite early. I
watched them giving their twin youngsters, Harry and Mary,
some spending money at Disneyland one summer day. "Here's
two dollars apiece," they were told. "Get something to take
home to Grandma and Grandpa." It was a joy to watch them
hover around the counters trying to decide. First of all, it was
an adventure in teamwork, because two dollars does not buy
much today. And both of them felt they had to agree on the
other's purchase. The seven-year-olds spent considerable time
debating and measuring. Finally Grandpa got a jointly funded
Alpine hat with a feather and Grandma got an ornate teacup.
But the children had taken a valuable step in economic values.

In this matter of a child's growing autonomy, the child
should also be encouraged to get himself out of his own
difficulties, especially if they are problems at his own level.
Minor difficulties at school should be settled by the child
himself. When Jacqueline complains, "the teacher made me
miss recess today because she said I was talking during a test,"
the parent can simply say, "OK. Just remember that the
next time and don't do it anymore."

One of the matters causing greatest difficulty in the home is
that of freedom to choose friends. Here the parent has
already provided subtle but meaningful guidance through the
years. The youngster's tastes in recreation, books, and clothing
have already been established by earliest childhood. But
unless the neighbor's child is literally a criminal, your boy or
girl should have the privilege of choosing companions. Most
parents may notice that their children eventually choose
companions matching their family tastes—although not
always.

Friend choices will often be made on very superficial
rationale. "Hey, Dad, you should see my new friend with bubble

gum. He can blow a bubble as big as his head!" Your tolerant relaxation and even enthusiastic response to such friends will help the child through an important phase of social life. Some guidance when a companion is actually dangerous can be done subtly enough and will probably be appreciated by the child. In fact, a firm, loving hand in these instances may frequently be a relief for the youngster. A wise parent can let him off the hook.

An overly severe type of control over a child, not allowing him to make his own decisions, will leave him a weakened person who cannot face later life. It is most difficult for a Christian youngster to make right decisions in adulthood if he has not smaller opportunities to do so in his home.

2. The *second trait of a good home* requires that the *parents be fairly well adjusted to their society or environment.* Or even if slightly maladjusted, at least they will not pass along such to their child. Because a mother is afraid of lightning, she should make a special effort not to display it in front of Malcolm or Miriam, her preschoolers.

It is more difficult in the later years to break ingrained fears that have been set since childhood. One may know intellectually that a certain fear is irrational and unwarranted, but his ornery subconscious persists. Fear of speaking in public is a common phobia that can be aggravated by an unthinking parent or teacher.

Jane, for example, had a slight stammering difficulty at age five deriving from a moderately unstable family. She recalls, "When company was at our house for dinner, I tried to join the conversation. I would get just so far before I struck a speech snag. My father would make me go back to the beginning of the sentence and start again and again. Finally I would get up and run from the table. To this day, words often stick in my throat even when I speak to a small group."

Such speech problems in a family setting must be dealt with in kindness and patience. The best help for Jane would have been counseling by a speech therapist.

"Today," relates Jane, "I cannot even read a passage from the Bible aloud to my husband unless I pray about it first. My third-grade teacher used to make me stand and read selections from my text aloud to the class. I dreaded those times so much that I became physically ill and had to be excused to the girls' room, where I threw up my meals. As I think back, I remember that my mother had similar speech problems. And I notice it slightly now in one of my children."

Warm-hearted counseling plus acceptance by an understanding family will make a difference in such situations. Jane also relates the most significant cure: "When I have to speak before a ladies' group at church, I just place it in the Lord's hands. I pray, 'Lord, this is your meeting and I am your child. Touch my lips and deliver your message through them.' It is the most amazing experience of 'surrender' and I find that only then can I go through the meeting without a hitch."

Such phobias are weakened only by love and understanding as they are coupled with reasoning. Condemnation will drive them deeper and often exaggerate them. Long-lasting and irrational guilt can pursue the child through the years. Faith and Bible quotations should not be used in a negative sense or to create neurotic dread.

How many parents have warned children not to mimic their elders, even in fun, for fear God will punish them as Elisha did with bears in 2 Kings 2:23, 24? Or how many have threatened a child with the words, "and all liars shall have their part in the lake which burneth with fire and brimstone"? True, this is in the Word of God, but should be discussed with the young child only in the setting of a gospel of love. Our faith is not a weapon against our children, but a cradle of grace.

Probably as damaging as any device is the statement, "Jane, your faith cannot be very great if you are afraid. No Christian should ever be afraid!" Many complex guilt problems develop from such injunctions. The Scripture is filled with evidence that the Christian life is a journey through a fear-infested world to which everyone is prey, and for whom God's presence is the only defense.

3. The *third trait* of a good home is that the children will be *provided with good models for living.* For the young child, especially at an early age, the parent alone remains the ideal pattern since he identifies most closely with mother or father.

This identification will manifest itself in some way throughout the remainder of the child's life. A boy will ordinarily model himself and his ambitions after his father. Often he will choose the same or a similar profession as he goes through life. The mother will be the girl's model. When later she becomes a businesswoman, a professional, a housewife and mother, the same patterns, attitudes, and habits will probably be hers. Most of the child's ideas about home life and marriage are derived from his home. These will later be applied to his home life a generation hence.

Jun Choon, one of our Korean girls, illustrated this beautifully as she traveled through life: "I was born in Jaeju City, the oldest in a good Christian home of four children. My father ran a small factory there and supported us very nicely. I was a happy little girl. However, misfortune befell our family when I was still very young," she wrote us. "I was only in the third grade when my dear father who loved us so much became bedridden with what proved to be a fatal disease. He lingered for three years and it was terrible to watch him waste away. It was also hard for the family in a material way because we sank deeply into debt without our breadwinner. Our house and furniture were eventually sold to pay our bills. After Father's death, Mother and we four children were hungry very often.

"At last, Mother decided to set up a small business selling vegetables from a peddler's stand. It was very hard and we were frequently cold and threadbare. But thankfully, God's light began to shine on our family when a friend introduced us to the Jaeju Widows' and Children's Home. I feel that it was God's hand that led us there when we were most desperate.

"I was just finishing sixth grade at that time and you were able to help me enter junior high school. How blessed I was to become a member of your family at that important time in my life. As I sat at my desk that first day I remember praying, 'Lord, thank you for not forsaking my family!' During the four years that we received help from the widows' home, Jesus Christ became deeply rooted in my heart. Eventually I finished high school and was able to enter Jaeju Teachers' College with a scholarship which you helped to provide.

"By God's help my mother was able to find a better position and our family was finally able to stand on its own. I remember so clearly the little prayer meeting we had when the four other members of our home sent me off to college: 'Lord, you have been so faithful. Continue to watch over us.'

"In 1973 when I was twenty-two years old, I was married to a wonderful man. Now we have two sons and I am a happy housewife. Also, I am a head teacher in the local primary school with sixty children to teach. My husband came to know the Lord shortly after we were married, and on Sundays we attend church faithfully with our two boys."

The aspects of wrong modeling can be seen in a young woman referred to by Paul Tournier in *The Person Reborn*. Here, too, a child's father had disappeared while she was still tiny, causing great anger and rebellion against God. Despite the fact that she was a pious person and faithful churchgoer, she could not believe in his goodness. "Basically," she said, "I am afraid of God. My difficulty in believing in God the *Father* stems from the fact that I do not know what a real father is like."

She relates that when she was still very little, after her father left home, she had repeated nightmares about his coming to carry her away. In her childhood, she says, her idea of a father was that of a monster. "Later on," she continues, "I was terrified of my stepfather's riding whip and being locked in my room on a diet of bread and water." In her early teens, if she misbehaved her mother would "threaten to send me back to my real father. I felt at that time as though God had deserted me. I was always afraid."

Fritz Kunkel in his *Search for Maturity* says, "The very young child cannot distinguish between parents and God at first. To him (infancy to two or three years old) they *are* God. The love for man and love for God (at that age) are identical. He accepts them as they are and applies what he learns from them to life and to mankind and to God. They are his only knowledge of religion. *Here is where religious education begins*. If we destroy the early we-feeling of our children, we destroy the basis of their religious life. *If we are bad parents the young child learns that God is bad!*"

Of course, as Christians we know that rebirth can restructure our thinking and good Christian counseling can help immensely. But scars remain.

4. The *fourth trait* of a good home is to make it an *interesting, exciting, and stimulating place* for the child to grow up. Surrounded by good books, games, and music the child will want to spend as much time there as he can. He will want to invite his friends there often. He will be proud of it. It need not be a mansion nor have a swimming pool. But it will be a place of good fellowship and warm acceptance.

Madame Ernestine Schuman-Heink, the great opera singer, once wrote:

What is a home?
A roof to keep out the rain?
Walls to keep out the wind?
Floors to keep out the moisture?
A home is more than that.
It is the laughter of a child,
The song of a mother,
The strength of a father,
The warmth of loving hearts,
Light from happy eyes,
Kindness, loyalty, comradeship.
Home is the first school,
And the first church
Where they learn about a loving God,
What is right, what is good,
And what is kind.
Where they go for comfort
When they are hurt or sick.
Where joy is shared and sorrow eased;
Where fathers and mothers,
Are respected and loved;
Where children are wanted.
Where the simplest food is good enough for kings
Because it is earned;
Where money is not so important as lovingkindness

Where even the teakettle sings for happiness.
That is a home.

Thus having examined the various patterns of family life, we find that we can examine supportive aid a child needs as he moves into more autonomous roles. The following chapter will attempt to deal with identity formations in a child's later life as he increasingly faces the world.

SEVEN
SUPPORTING HIM AS
HE MEETS THE WORLD

Socializing the child begins on the day of his birth. Earliest impressions of the child remain for a lifetime.

John G. Paton, the first great missionary to the New Hebrides, relates his father's childhood influence on him: "If everything else in my religion were by some accident blotted out, my soul would go back to those early days." John related how as a boy he would crouch by his father's door listening to him praying for John by name. "God was so real to him," he wrote in later life, "that he became real to me. His prayers were answered in me.

"For sixty years my father kept up the practice of family prayer. None of us can remember one single day ever passing without being hallowed by prayer. No hurry for business, or market, or sorrow, no joy or excitement ever prevented us from kneeling while my father, the family high priest, offered himself, his wife and his children to God." Such guidance echoed through this missionary's lifetime of social and spiritual contribution.

GUIDELINES

In such a home a child can learn that his feelings remain uniquely his. Seven guidelines for a parent can help him from babyhood:

1. The child should feel that he is respected and understood as an individual.

2. That people care about him and will take care of him.

3. That he has a true home where he belongs and can stay.

4. That his parents can tolerate his unacceptable behavior and can still love him without rejecting him as a person, even though he needs correction.

5. That he can depend on his parents for protection and guidance in controlling his impulses until he is old enough to establish his own controls over them.

6. That he has someone to help him with his problems in the group, at school, in the community, and elsewhere.

7. That he has someone who can share his dreams and work with him in moving toward his future goals.

That these childhood feelings are not always observed is only too apparent as one studies the life style of many families. A London newspaper in the 1950s conducted a survey of the emotions of 100,000 children. Among those polled were youngsters from many countries as well as England. From the replies the paper derived a "decalogue of commandments for parents":

1. Don't quarrel in front of your children.

2. Treat all your children with equal love.

3. Never lie to your child.

4. Let there be mutual love between the parents.

5. Let there be friendship and comradeship between parents and child.

6. Treat your children's friends as welcome guests.

7. Always answer children's questions.

8. Don't punish your child in front of others.

9. Concentrate on your child's good points. Don't harp on his failings.

10. Be constant in your affections and moods.

And the children, by common consent, added one for good measure (and the most important):

11. Treat your child as a sacred trust from God.

Many children sent gratuitous comments. And one little girl sent hers concerning the first commandment in the form of a prayer: "Dear God, please keep Mom and Dad from quarreling so much."

IDENTITY FORMATION

As the child moves away from early teens, his adjustment is often labeled "identity formation."

1. At this time, the child is looking for a new separateness. A child is afraid that he or she will be swept up and handcuffed to views of an earlier generation. He feels he needs to take direct steps to assure himself there is a part of him that is not totally reflecting his parents and their views. During the early years away from home—often at college—he may still tend to cling to parental manners and customs. Slowly, however, he begins to move away from the parent as a model and starts to fashion his own identity. Sometimes this occurs with traumatic suddenness.

Myra, a six-year-old girl in India, was placed in a foster home because her parents were very poor and already had sixteen children when she was born. Unfortunately she still lived near her old home and knew who her real parents were. She constantly wandered away and back to her parental household hoping that they might change their mind.

"It broke my heart over and over," she told me, "until finally when I was ten, I made up my mind that if they didn't want me, I wouldn't want them. For the first time I had peace of mind about it. I just went about the task of growing up with my 'new' parents. Now I am twenty and engaged to be married."

Although not always such an obvious ambivalence in many young persons, it is often reached slowly and painfully. Back of it all, we feel that our parents are gazing over our shoulders, anxious to indicate our failings. Each time they reject us there is resentment and bewilderment. Each time they uphold us there is a warmth of approval tinged with some irritation. The child, halfway between dominance and autonomy, asks himself, "Am I pursuing my own direction in life or am I merely confirming their ideals? Am I just continuing to be a good boy for their sake?"

Particularly happy are parents who can light their child with love of adventure and sense of risk, different from their own perhaps strictured lives. Tournier makes the comment in his *Adventure of Living,* "How dull are the lives of children who are spoiled, so that they lose all ambition and weary of everything!"

Henri Bergson, as a young philosopher at the turn of the century, experienced this inner struggle for novelty. He said, "I have just given my publisher a manuscript and it is worthless. What I have said in it that is new is not interesting. And what I have said that is interesting is not new!" But he was experiencing what every young person must pass through if he is not to be a counterfeit.

2. "Identity formation" is the designation we convey to the development of the child's self during his adolescence. The boy or girl is confronting the opinions of a parent and must evaluate in his own terms and fit them to the world he knows. He must work out his own freedoms by challenging his childhood axioms. He must be a partner with others, comparing and rejecting opinions, testing continually. Later he may surrender many of these new-gained liberties to a lifetime mate. He tries his wings in areas in which his parents have never ventured. He comes back to earth, and his father challenges his wisdom. He feels quashed but soon takes off again in another direction with his comrades, to experience new attachments. He lands and his father again challenges his lovely new hypotheses. He has to study and know the differences between his new companions and his father. If he is to exercise his true spiritual freedom, all future choices must now be his and his alone.

How many Christian parents have sent their child to a university in fear and trembling? Will he remain true to his faith? Will he resist temptations? Will he make the right friends? Will he choose the right course? Will he marry the right girl? Every child, if his life is to be real, must now know this dimension of risk. Dr. Roger Gould reminds us, "If we tie ourselves too closely to the illusion of absolute safety and do not take risks necessary to emancipate ourselves from childhood consciousness, we live a dull life without full adult consciousness!"

Having spent eighteen years in family intimacy with each of our children, my wife and I have said as each went off to college, "We have done all we can. His life now belongs to God and himself. We trust that our Christian upbringing will bear fruit, in God's way, not ours."

Some years back I knew a John Gabel who had been reared in a Christian home. But, as often occurs, he fought bitterly with his father during his mid-teens. Eventually he ran away at age seventeen and became involved in drugs and alcohol in the San Francisco area of Haight-Ashbury. In time his habits caused what seemed to be total blindness. Taken to a downtown hospital, he was visited providentially by a local pastor who was able to learn a bit of his history. Slowly and gently John was led back to a loving relationship with God. And over a period of time his eyesight was partially restored.

Thankfully, most children's identity formation period is not so painful as John's. But the entire upbringing of each child is usually designed as a series of precautions to avoid risks such as this. Even though society is rapidly changing, the aim stays constant: Socialization is a game, and our children need to know how it is played. But it requires a steadfast home.

So much depends on this emotional and spiritual stability of the parents. Studies at Harvard, for example, seem to indicate major roots of delinquency among teenagers:

6 out of every 10 delinquents have fathers who drink excessively.

4 out of 10 have mothers who also drink to excess.

3 out of 4 delinquents are allowed to come and go as they please, with no questions asked by parents.

7 out of 10 are from homes where there is no family recreation.

3 out of 5 are from homes where there is discord between parents.

4 out of 5 have parents who are hostile or indifferent to their children's friends.

4 out of 5 say their mothers are indifferent to them personally.

3 out of 5 delinquents report that their fathers are indifferent.

4 out of 10 come from broken homes.

1 out of 10 gets religious training of any kind.

Linda Goldfarb, authority in child care, reports some conversations with teachers showing how smaller children have high degrees of discernment: "Even an eight-year-old understands what's happening if a parent cheats, or keeps too much change given by a sales clerk ...."

"If grownups use bad language, or lie, or cheat or show disrespect for the law in front of their children, what can they expect of their youngsters?"

3. Parents need to establish a platform of success for their children. They especially need to define "success" in social, moral, and emotional terms, not simply in the worldly guidelines of material attainment.

Dr. William Glasser says that children need "a chance to succeed, a chance for involvement and a chance to do something worthwhile." His book, *Identity Society,* distinguishes two well-defined types of people: those with failure identities and those with identities of success. People who from childhood have been imbued with an inner success image can take amazing amounts of stress.

Dr. Glasser defines certain "companions" that people use in positive proportion to their sense of failure. These "companions" include such things as alcohol, drugs, tranquilizers, barbiturates, and similar crutches. Interestingly he also adds some so-called psychosomatic problems to be included among the "companions." Such diseases as stomach ulcers, colitis, asthma, chronic back pain, headaches, and eczema are listed by him (and other doctors) as "companions" that exonerate the patient from failures. "A faithful ulcer," he says, "will gain a doctor's attention, easy access to drugs to relieve the suffering, and fashionable acceptance by others who have or respect ulcers." Sadly, he adds that "ulcers are common in children as well as in adults." The rejected child, the "used" child, and the abused child are among those that resort to ulcers as companions. And further, "adults who as children had stomach ulcers will probably choose the same symptom when confronted with loneliness and failure."

A well-adjusted parent can help his or her child build a success-identity. The child needs to learn assertiveness without displaying anger or other emotions. He "catches" this from his parent more than he learns through verbalizing. The child should learn to express displeasure when he is passed over in a "treat" by being able to express logically what he has done to deserve it. Later in life when he gets passed over for a raise, he can go to the boss with equanimity or even in controlled anger and request his just deserts. The person with the failure-identity will more likely have learned to be depressed and not mention it to his superior.

It is a truism and a commentary on our society that the more successful the parent the more successful his child, all other things being equal. The child with the success-identity grows by each new experience into a new level of achievement. The feelings of fulfillment pyramid into attitudes of further accomplishment. It becomes a cycle: the more capably he performs, the better he feels about himself. The better he feels about himself, the more capably he performs.

Song Kyung Hee was brought to the Moo Doong Orphanage when he was seven. His Christian home had been completely destroyed by a bomb and he was left without a living relative. The father, according to the record, had been a Christian in his village with a notable success-identity as a leader. The report on Kyung Hee indicates that he was at first assigned to the chore of caring for the orphanage piglets. It was his duty to watch over the baby pigs and clean their pen regularly. "He kept it as clean as glass," the superintendent wrote to us. "At age nine he began measuring and weighing the piglets daily, and kept careful records. As boys will, his companions ridiculed Kyung Hee but it made no difference, for they could not dissuade him."

The boy's memory of his father's attention to detail continued to influence him into his junior and senior high school experiences. Although it was especially hard for him as he entered high school (competition for a desk was intense), "nevertheless he continued to perform his chores diligently," continued the superintendent. "He insisted on studying late into the night. At times he stayed up much too late and eventually it affected his health. I recall how he suffered from nose bleeds and anemia." Eventually, he finished high school in Chon Ra with highest honors and was admitted as a pre-med student at Chon Nam University where he continued to attain top grades.

His Christian training, not only in the orphanage but from early childhood, continued to have long-range effects. Although he studied late into the night, he also devoted himself to formation and leadership of a Christian student union on campus. "It was his dream to become a doctor and care for poor people," the superintendent told us. Later in medical school he followed the same habit pattern in the laboratory after hours—often until midnight. Although he had little leisure time, he devoted himself to regular responsibility at his Christian campus meetings. "Often," said his mentor, "he devoted himself to campaigns raising money for poor people in our community."

After graduation he met a lovely nurse, was married, and presently enjoys a happy family life with several children. But as ever "the tape continues to run." He is now a physician serving the poor, as well as teaching struggling medical and nursing students.

Dr. Leslie Weatherhead, noted pastoral counselor and longtime minister of London's City Temple, tells about a non-achiever who sat next to him in school when he was a boy. "All of life is a school," he mused, "and how do we expect to get through school without examinations?" He reminisces about his boyhood study times. "I remember my school days," he writes. "I hated them. I dreaded them. I feared them." And to add to the gall, young Leslie sat next to a boy named "Fatty" Jones. "Fatty had the most 'wonderful' father in the world," recalls Weatherhead. "If the sun shone too hot, his father didn't care whether Fatty came to school or not. If there were exams, my friend Fatty could escape them and play." It was a bitter experience. "My 'cruel' father expected me to go to school whether it rained or shined. If there were exams I had to attend and pass." Today it doesn't look so bad. "I know now which was the finer father," he recalls, "and who showed the greater love. How do we expect to get away without the tests of life?"

4. Parents teach a child about *alternative modes and moods* in achieving success-identity or failure-identity.

I clearly remember losing my temper one day in a public restaurant when my son was about seven years of age. It was over poor service and a spilled glass by a waiter. I was about to burst, when my wife calmed me with a look. "Oh rats," David remarked, "I wanted to see Daddy get mad." I suddenly realized how much a son occasionally needs to see how his father handles frustrations. There are success and failure methods of handling them. Success persons know when to be aggressive or assertive. They also know how to do it without a paralyzing anger that minimizes effective handling. They know too how to assert rights without flaring into a destructive dispute. Under attack they know how to respond with understanding, thus diverting another's aggression.

Successful parents can teach how to deal with temper and other manifestations of negative emotion by converting and channeling them into positive terms. Basically they have taught themselves and now lead their children in methods that will convert tensions into holistic growth. They guide their youngsters into pleasurable emotions that can, if properly handled, stem from negative situations. Basically it is done through deeper involvement in the lives of others. For the person who angers us, we can say, "Let's see how we can solve this problem together."

I believe it was Samuel Johnson who in talking to his biographer Boswell remarked, "Do you see that man over there?" indicating another with his cane. "I hate that man!" "But," protested Boswell, "you don't even know him." "Yes," replied Johnson, "that's why I hate him." His point was that those we know superficially we do not like. Only as we know and relate to them in depth do we learn to love and cooperate with them.

Ken Kesey's book *One Flew Over the Cuckoo's Nest* raises some negative aspects concerning questions of morality. But these are far outweighed by its feeling for humanity and compassion. The hero, named Mac, is a young man erroneously committed to a psychopathic ward who flagrantly disregards rigid hospital rules in order to reach the hearts and emotions of his fellow inmates. It is a moving experience to see one after another opening to his enthusiastic ploys for communication. The most touching is his relation to a seven-foot Indian whom he calls "Chief." Chief is catalogued as a deaf-mute, semi-catatonic, who mops the floor in a zombie-like trance. Mac, however, will not accept him as that. He talks to him, although others scold him for it. He involves him in a wild basketball game against the attendants by placing Chief by the goal with hands upraised to deflect the ball into the basket for a score. Eventually, through continued involvement, Chief begins to talk and open up. It confirms the old cliché— we cannot label and "thingify" people and expect to experience true communication with them.

Helping a child to live with the ambiguities of life is one of the difficult tasks of parenthood. The tensions often cause regression and outright retreat. Indeed, people of adult age have the same problems: love and hate, acceptance and rejection, joy and sadness, and many other alternatives often catch people by surprise. They lead some people, especially at identity-crisis age, to reject the values and the faith of previous generations. Inevitably each person must face cosmic questions of personal destiny and meaning.

Each triumph we experience brings to our minds the statement of Napoleon's mother, "Provided it lasts!" The animal kingdom does better physically than mankind. They have worked out a balance of survival, keeping warm, eating, sleeping, mating. They do not see themselves in the context of sweeping history. "Man," said one humanist, "is the only animal who knows he will die!"

Man, too, is the only creature who can have all the accoutrements of outward achievement and yet feel miserable. A man may have his name in lights, be listed in *Who's Who*, and be worth a million. Yet he may ultimately say to himself, "I really blew it. What a mess my life has been." In his memory bank he has recorded his failures, inhumanities, mistakes, and lost chances for better ways. A gloom pervades Western man, and in his quiet moments he asks, "Is this all there is?" Our dream world records our sense of shortcoming. The nighttime is alive with examinations for which we are not prepared, sermons we cannot preach, planes we have missed, dark shadows at the top of the stairs.

Life decisions boil down to ultimate solutions—God versus no-God. Camus was an atheist existentialist who concluded for himself, "Life is an endless cycle revolving forever without meaning." On the other hand, Arnold Toynbee, while agreeing with a cyclical view of history, said, in effect, that everything in personal and world history has a meaning with a beginning and ending, and God is involved in a cosmic enterprise which includes every man, woman and child. At a more personal level, Ignatius Loyola gave voice to a parent's most gratifying goal: "We must make no decision without opening our hearts to love!" And of course Scripture goes on to remind us that the love of God is shed abroad in our hearts by the Holy Spirit.

5. Parents can help a child's growth by assisting at *severing the emotional cord*. The cord starts early in life—in fact at birth—with the bonding between mother and child. That earliest relationship lasts forever. But there are ways that a parent can ease his child toward autonomy whenever possible. In his mid-teens, George dangles between childhood and adulthood. At eighteen or nineteen he is suspended in limbo. He is not really a boy any longer, and yet he is not an adult. From sixteen to twenty-two he will pass through this most difficult time. He must begin to build an adult identity for himself, but in order to do this, he must now begin seeing his parents as fallible humans.

The weight of a parent's influence is hardest on George at this particular hiatus. A slight hint of criticism from his father can send George into a tirade. His ego is at its most brittle during this six-year period since he is so unsure of his identity. It is hard for George to look on Mother and Dad as typical well-intentioned adults, which is probably what they are. They attend church, give to charities, vote regularly, accept social conventions, operate in an acceptable routine. But of course, like most people in the world they are confused by rapid twentieth-century changes, by changing moral patterns, and by swirling technical advances. If George can see them as good-hearted, often erring, loving but normally prejudiced people, he has been helped toward maturity.

It is hard for Mother and Dad to change, for it threatens their very existence. But George, as a member of his own identity-passage, feels that he must attempt to alter their ways and their thoughts. It is so essential to him because instinctively he realizes that if he can change them, he can change himself. Problems in them are basically the same problems that are in him. Throughout his life he has been taught to ingest or "swallow" them—their values, their habits, their mannerisms, their faith. Now to be a true adult he must have all these transmogrified as his own, with all necessary variations to make them special.

6. The parent should remind himself ceaselessly, "My *child's person is more important than his purpose.*" Too many mothers and fathers confuse the worth of their child with his ability to succeed. It is far more important that they emphasize repeatedly, "What you are is much more vital to me than what you *do!*" Much of our society today measures people by what we can derive from them—what they can do for us. "What's in it for me?" should not be the philosophy in a Christian home.

The parent's stress should be "I love you, my son, for yourself. You must decide your personal goals for yourself." This requires a deep sense of involvement between parent and child.

Jacqueline Cochran, the pioneer aviatrix in the early days of flying, was born in a poverty-stricken family in the cypress swamps of Florida. Only a relative who believed in her kept her on the track of a personal goal. Other than that, she had no home life, little education. She had no shoes until she was eight. Yet she fought her way up to become a pioneer air pilot. The goal of flying was planted in her early. As she says in her autobiography, "Flying got into my soul immediately, but the reason why must be found in the mystic maze of my birth and childhood and the early circumstances of my life." The beginning of it all was in a rustic shack on Sawdust Road. "I might have been born in a hovel, but I early determined to travel with the wind and the stars!"

A goal like this can be encouraged by adults but should not be manipulated. This, if strongly felt and watered by warm showers of loving acceptance, is the one that will move toward a desired goal. Charles told his mother, "I want to be a writer when I grow up!" to which she replied, "Oh you can do better than that. Everyone has wanted to be a writer at some time or other!" He eventually did write several books and many monographs, and perhaps even the mother's negative note became a challenge. Sometimes a child needs some opposition as a superable obstacle. But it needs to be tempered with a deep knowledge of a child's defeat-quotient.

Hebrews says, "Obviously no 'chastening' seems pleasant at the time ... Yet when it is all over we can see that it has quietly produced the fruit of real goodness in the characters of those who have accepted it in the right spirit" (12:11, Phillips).

The next thing a parent can do to shore up a child's personal goal is to work together with him so that he can experience some seedling success toward achievement. Sometimes this will mean helping him sort out good from bad in his approaches. An unknown writer has encouraged nurturing:

"I must not interfere with my child; I am told not to help him shape himself through some mold of thought. 'Naturally as a flower,' it is said, 'he must unfold.' Yet even flowers have discipline of wind and rain. And though I know it gives a gardener pain, I've seen him using pruning shears to give strength and beauty to the blossoms. Only weeds unfold naturally."

Thus, with acceptance of the child's own goal, the parent should pitch in but let the successes be the youngster's and his alone. When they browse through stores looking for a child's tools (and if the budget allows) some choices should be the child's. As he or she molds his goal, even at a tender age, even tiny successes will seem like exciting masterpieces.

Added to this will be responsibilities around the home that support feelings of achievement and acceptance. Chores that a child enjoys should be encouraged. Small payment for harder ones can give a sense of attainment. Success-identity children may need emoluments less than do underachievers. But above all, success should not be measured in money, fame, or power. It should be governed by a child's inner consciousness of fulfillment.

Having this satisfaction quotient in one's life is a vital step toward accepting others for what they are. The achievement-oriented child will be the best equipped to experience rapport with people of every socioeconomic level, race, religion, or the opposite sex.

In one of her last newspaper columns, Dorothy Thompson related her feelings about her father and his influence on people from every walk of life: "In worldly terms, he was not a successful man. But the goodness of his character, his spirit, his love of beauty, his allergy to everything tawdry or cheap, his quiet intolerance of evil; the broadness of his humanity, his patience; his simple and profound faith that recognized Christ as a continual presence and example moved everyone with whom he came in contact. I cannot imagine that evil-doers, materialistic communists, or any negative force would have gotten anywhere within the radius of his influence."

Here was a man who exemplified SUCCESS in its truest form. In the next chapter we will explore the subjects of interpersonal relationships at their optimum without regard to artificial barriers society often imposes.

EIGHT
GUIDING HIM IN
SOCIAL RELATIONSHIPS

"How can I teach my child to make friends in a mobile country composed largely of minority groups?" one parent asked me. It is such a common problem that Vance Packard has written a book on the subject: *A Nation of Strangers.* Alvin Toffler in his volume *Future Shock* has seen this alienation as a major issue in our "brave new society." "Besides losing their attachment to things and places," he says in his 1970 research, "people are also becoming less involved with other individuals." He deplores the superficiality of our day and adds, "Rather than relating to the total personality of another person, the individual today maintains a superficial and partial contact with most people he encounters!"

Although that be true in the secular world, how tragic when it occurs in the society of the church. As a pastor of twenty years, I watched many families break up in divorce, much of it predicated on a creeping alienation of one party from the other. In one church on Long Island their Christian friends watched helplessly as one of our leading couples drifted apart. Jane began to let her face and figure go, although she remained outgoing and busy about the church. Charles wandered away from the church and made friends among gambling and drinking companions. One day he stunned her by calling long distance to say that he was not coming home anymore. He had found another woman with whom he "was truly in love."

It needs to be underscored that family life is the *root of all friendships.* If a husband and wife are not truly each other's friends and their children's, there is trouble ahead. It is from the family's nuclear friend-making skill that all other friendships are born.

In Jane's case, the divorce was such a blow that she slowly withdrew from her Christian friends. "I was a small package wrapped up in myself," she confessed. "I felt rejected by my society, because Charles had rejected me." Loneliness followed, and then isolation. It was only by our encouraging her reinvolvement that she finally, after two years, drew back into the joys of Christian community.

Frieda Fromm Reichman states, "People are more frightened of being lonely than of being hungry or of being deprived of sleep, or of having sexual needs unfulfilled." Loneliness, when it becomes unbearable, can drive a person into derangement.

My wife often remarks about our travels, "I find the people I meet far more interesting than the places!" People worldwide are seeking fulfillment, a feeling of personal value and, above all, acceptance by others. So, too, are our children.

For them we must not erect barriers around ourselves. We must break down walls and build bridges. Hugh Prather once said, "For communication to have meaning, it must have a life. It must transcend 'you and me' and become 'us.' When I meet another person I see in him some unique thing that is not me. And he sees something in me that is not resident in himself." This is doubtless the meaning of the Communion—"I partake a bit of you. And you partake a bit of me. And we both partake of a common Lord!" This all grows into FELLOWSHIP and we must be glad and willing to BE what develops from that.

ON MAKING FRIENDS

A child must be led to know the art of introducing himself. It comes basically, of course, from watching Mother and Dad do it over a twenty-year period. But it is also a skill. One's demeanor, one's affirmative self-concept, one's pride in appearance, one's education and inflection, all of these can lead into a positive action-dialogue with a new acquaintance.

Bach and Deutsch in their book *Pairing* have indicated that when two persons find a potential friend in each other they desire to gain insight quickly as to the kind of intimate he or she will make. They attempt to know one another's genuine self.

Every normal child from a reasonably normal family already has a ready-installed friend-making packet. It involves many things that people like Dale Carnegie have been teaching through the years:

Get the conversation going. This is Rule Number One and there is no substitute.

Demonstrate real concern about the other's feelings and views.

Sometimes take a risk in striking up acquaintances. Don't always be afraid of rejection. Winston Churchill once said, "Courage is the first of human qualities, because it is the quality which guarantees all others."

Realize that others have the same desire for friendship. Everyone is searching for fellowship and closeness.

The other person will react more favorably if you are honest and direct.

Don't worry about how you look. When you are into conversation, don't check your tie or hair, or look at your watch. Total devotion to the other's words and interests is the watchword.

A smile from time to time lights up the dialogue.

Insert into the conversation some highlights about yourself that will reveal your underlying personality.

Dr. and Mrs. Leonard Zunin have written a challenging book entitled *Contact, The First Four Minutes*. In it they point out the four Cs that are essential to making friends. They are helpful to parent and child alike:

1. *Confidence* in yourself.
2. *Creativity* in what you say.
3. *Caring*—give four minutes of your *total* attention.
4. *Consideration* for the other person as an individual.

In one of my first books, written over twenty years ago, *Help Your Boy or Girl to Be Christian,* I suggested some basic things that children might remember in this vital area of friend-making. Believing they are still valid today, I list them below:

1. Help children to understand—and thus to like—all kinds of people.

2. Encourage children to take a *genuine* interest in other folks.

3. Give them many and varied contacts with different sorts of people, by inviting them to the home and visiting in other homes.

4. Encourage children to bring friends home to play as well as to visit in other homes.

5. Assist your young people in developing skills that will make them attractive to their contemporaries. Skills like piano playing, trumpet playing, ball playing, and the like will go a long way toward forming natural and lasting friendships.

6. Don't prevent children from wearing clothes that are the "in thing" with their group—unless, of course, rudimentary decency prohibits.

7. Teach children the principles of proper introduction of friends to one another and to adults.

8. Even in this permissive and relaxed age, cleanliness is still important in making friends.

ON HANDLING REJECTION

Probably the fear of rejection is one of the greatest obstacles to friendships. Some of our child-care work takes place in South Africa in enclaves that make up segregated countries such as Lesotho and Swaziland. There among the Babembas we have observed a custom that illustrates a gentle method of social suasion. When someone performs a reprehensible or unfair deed, he is not punished in the normal sense of the word. There are no jails, no whipping posts, and no penalties. The one who has committed the crime is placed in the center of his village, isolated but untied. The villagers stop their labors and all members of the community join together forming a large circle about the guilty one. Then every member of the Babemba community begins in turn to "affirm" the accused. Each tells all the good things he knows about the person, all the kind things he has done, all the fine skills he possesses. The children as well as the grownups take part. Every happening each one can recall is recited with as much detail as possible. Nothing negative is recited; only the person's good and kind and generous actions are related. No jokes, exaggerations, or fabrications are allowed, only the truth.

Sometimes the observance continues for days and does not stop until each person is satisfied that he has recalled everything he can. At the end a great banquet is held and the erring one is received back into the bosom of the tribe, fully forgiven and restored.

It is an occasion very similar to that of the prodigal who "came to himself" after deep self-searching and was received back by his father with great rejoicing.

It would be ideal if each Christian community could experience this kind of acceptance and full forgiveness. It would open the door to the rejected, the minorities, the downtrodden of the world, to whom the Savior was always receptive.

Years ago when my wife and I were just starting out in the pastorate, we had occasion to be in New York visiting Radio City. It was a crowded season and we stopped in at Child's Restaurant for ice cream. The shop was jammed with people, but we noticed a happy-looking couple occupying one end of a long table, in laughing conversation.

"May we join you folks at the other end of the table?" we asked.

"Certainly not!" snapped the lady. "This is a private table."

We moved on and soon found a more congenial couple that we could join, and made some very good friends. But for some reason the demoralized feeling of that singular rejection stays with me through the years. It taught me never to accept an initial rebuff. Had we been more timid or more unsure of ourselves, we might have withdrawn altogether and brooded on it. When faced with rejection by certain members of society, it is reaffirming for a child or young person to remind himself of the many places he is still accepted and loved.

Dr. John Powell in his helpful book *Why Am I Afraid to Tell You Who I Am?* indicates some of the inner feeling of many of us, fearful of rejection. "There is some communication of my person" in all of this, he says. He confesses that he is willing to take the initial step out of "solitary confinement" revealing of his sentiments and ideas. But he watches to make sure his companion is accepting him. If the listener narrows his eyes, raises his brows, yawns, or looks at his watch, then the speaker "retreats to safer ground." The child needs to be strengthened beforehand to meet these moments of repudiation and move on. Soon he will find success and acceptance.

ON ACCEPTING THE UNACCEPTED

One of the exciting experiences of the past few years has been the openness of homes to children of another color resulting from the fall of southeast Asia. In 1975 many of us were involved in what came to be called "Operation Baby Lift." It involved loading scores of tiny homeless babies aboard chartered planes in Cambodia and Vietnam and shuttling them to anxious families in Australia, Canada, and the United States.

One couple has experienced the joy of taking one of these youngsters, whom they renamed Nathan. He was only a year old when he came, young enough so that he had not absorbed Vietnamese culture to any noticeable degree. Marty and Karen Lonsdale of Whittier, California, already had a little three-year-old of their own named Lisa. How would it work out—a new son of another color and culture? "Wonderfully!" Marty and Karen say. "Do you ever have anyone stare at you when you take Nathan shopping?" "A few times," says Karen. "Some people ask me, 'What is he—Indian or Mexican?' " "Are they," I query, "just curious or are they unfriendly?" "A little of both," say the Lonsdales.

But most people close to them have been heartily supportive. The church that the Lonsdales attend is warmly affirming of little Nathan and his new family. A study by Rita J. Simon at the University of Illinois seems to indicate that only 9 percent of white adoptive couples have experienced negative reactions from friends or family; 25 percent were strongly approving, while over half were at least "neutral."

That Christians should be moving toward an increasingly open and understanding position on race relations need hardly be said. Paul's letter to the Colossians states, "In this new life one's nationality or race or education or social position is unimportant; such things mean nothing. Whether a person has Christ is what matters, and he is equally available to all" (3:11, TLB).

Albert Schweitzer was motivated by this same transracial call of God to go to Lambarene in Africa. In his book, *On the Edge of the Forest Primeval,* he describes his feelings after surgery on a black Christian brother suffering a painful disease. "The operation is finished in the hardly lighted dormitory. I watch the sick man's wakening." As the patient looks around he calls out, "I have no more pain—no more pain!" He feels around on the blanket and finds the doctor's hand. "He will not let me go," relates Schweitzer. "Then I say to him, 'The Lord Jesus has told me and my wife to come to the Ogowé people.' " The doctor and his patient sit there quietly thinking of these words. "And we," he concludes, "sit side by side and feel that we know by experience the meaning of the Lord's words, 'And you are all brethren.' "

ON SUPPORTING THE COMMUNITY TOWARD UNDERSTANDING

True friendships are only possible as they grow out of a wholesome home life. NEA vice-president Willard Mcguire says, "Violence, like charity, begins at home. It begins with the ugliness of poverty, inadequate food and heat, without books, and with inadequate communication."

In America, one out of six children now live in a single-parent home. Often both divorced parents reject their children after their separation. Last year 6,000 parents in Maryland alone voluntarily released custody of their offspring. Statistics in the same period record that two million youngsters were listed as "battered" children, brutally assaulted by their own parents. Most school children now come from homes in which both parents work, and no one supervises them after school. Often parents cannot even see them off properly in the morning.

Some communities have now begun intensive programs to

overcome childhood crime and supply emotional undergirding for young people. In Dade County, Florida, before such a program began there had been 10,000 cases of assault, theft, and vandalism during the school year 1974-1975. In the wealthy Miami Beach School where they have a school busing program bringing black youngsters to a predominantly white neighborhood, one incident was enough to turn the tide. After a black boy beat a white girl, an aroused public demanded action. Dr. Sam Moncur, director of the Opportunity Industrialization Center fostered a winning idea.

Dr. Moncur began what he termed a "Safe Schools" matrix of parent-counselors. These adults of both races were assigned to five racially mixed high schools, each with an average enrollment of 2,000 students.

Primarily, said Dr. Moncur, "We must establish law and order in the classroom and respect for property." Since the program's inception in October 1977, school attendance rose to 92 percent, a record. Delinquent or disruptive behavior went down by 72 percent. Vandalism fell off. Abusive language and fighting dropped off to practically nothing.

"I thought," said Dr. Moncur, "parents would take care of the problem if they were properly informed. Sure enough, it paid off."

On the other side of the nation in California's Santa Clara County, problems were occurring similar to those in Miami. Sociologists were predicting that Yerba Buena, a racially mixed school, would become the scene of the nation's most violent outbreak. Jerry Mullins, the principal, says today, "We were on top of the garbage heap!" But because of his positive program in student and community relations, the school is a model of decorum. Although over 50 percent of the student body are from welfare homes, Yerba Buena has risen from the country's worst school to the top 25 percent in orderliness and achievement. Mr. Mullins' program is worth examining because of its modeling potential for other communities.

First, Mr. Mullins ordered a formal evaluation to explore basic difficulties. The children's homes followed textbook descriptions of a poor home environment: bad relationships with fathers and mothers, unemployment, economic depression, negative self-concepts.

Second, the survey discovered a bureaucratic jungle in governmental youth services. Youngsters felt they were victims of an official shell-game in which they were jockeyed from one desk to another. He weathered normal resistance in order to reorganize and unify the youth service framework. Gone now is the constant lateral shuffle, and the young people receive quick response to their needs.

Third, he conceived an interagency federation for his children that brought service groups under a single jurisdiction at his school. Thus community and neighborhood assistance for the children work in unison with the police, social welfare, probation officers, and children's courts. Crisis intervention personnel were also introduced so that parents and children could receive immediate help when needed.

Fourth, parents' workshops and seminars were structured so that mothers and fathers could learn dynamics of warmer relationships with their children. "Discipline with empathy" was high on the list of subjects discussed.

The *San Francisco Chronicle,* in reporting the school's turnabout, said, "It is a new high school that is a model of harmony and achievement!"

Mr. Mullins himself stated with understandable satisfaction, "No group violence, no interracial disunity, no vandalism . . . it's a peaceful atmosphere."

Nothing is more relevant today than John Donne's famous sermon found in his 1624 *Devotions:* "Any man's death diminishes me, because I am involved in mankind. Therefore, never send to know for whom the bell tolls; it tolls for thee." Even more pertinent are the words from the epistle of James, "Dear brothers, how can you claim that you belong to the Lord Jesus Christ, the Lord of glory, if you show favoritism to rich people and look down on poor people?"

A child will learn these things only from a home that is warm and accepting—and color-blind.

ON INSPIRING A LOVE-VISION FOR ALL MANKIND

As he reads his Bible, a Christian knows that there is a world full of lonely people—sinners, yes, but people longing for a loving hand. They are filled with fears, contradictions, neuroses, and misconceptions. Only Christ is the answer.

It is his kind of love that has sent disciples through the ages into distant lands to proclaim the Good News. For them race, color, money, and personal ambition meant nothing.

In the New Hebrides there is a small island named Nguna. There over a hundred years ago was sent a young Christian named Peter Milne. It was a cannibal island when he arrived and he was instantly surrounded by sin, hatred, and suspicion. But Peter took the Lord with him and every day was a new adventure of his providence. He preached the gospel daily and eventually gave his life. Today Nguna is a Christian island and in the church that Milne founded, hangs a picture of himself. Under the portrait are these words, "When he came there was no light. When he died there was no darkness!"

One of the stories of our children that has impressed me through the years is that of Somatti. She was found years ago by a missionary named Clara Lerberg on a station platform in Jalgaon, India. Somatti was very little, stunted by malnutrition, Miss Lerberg recalled, and was only four years old. Ravenous with hunger, she was watching for an opportunity to beg for food. Miss Lerberg spied her from the window of her train as it stopped at the station. She beckoned to the youngster to climb aboard.

Timidly, Somatti climbed the steps just as the train began to move. The motion frightened her so much that she hid under one of the seats until Miss Lerberg persuaded her to come out.

The youngster could not speak either English or Marathi, the language of the area, but murmured in a strange tongue. When they arrived in Bombay, the authorities gave Miss Lerberg permission to keep the child.

The first job was to give Somatti a bath. The poor tot was encrusted with four years of filth and her hair was wild and unkempt. But she responded eagerly to affection, and the orphanage staff soon discovered she had an amazing intelligence. She learned to read and write, and moved quickly through the grades. Miss Lerberg was especially proud, too, of her physical appearance, especially in view of her frightful beginnings. She filled out beautifully with love and good food, and her hair became a luxuriant mass of curls.

Somatti's home and staff gave her the love that had been missing in her early years. An encouraging aspect of Reality Therapy is its affirmation that it is never too late. Dr. William Glasser in his book *Reality Therapy* says, "To avoid the issue of present behavior by searching for remote periods of loneliness or for rejections early in life . . . is wrong!" The Bombay Home provided Somatti with those small but daily successes so essential to her recovery from childhood trauma. When she evidenced symptoms of regression, they allowed her to ventilate these, but surrounded her with the warm, accepting climate that allowed her to overcome them and move on into a new success identity.

Somatti stayed at the home until she was twenty, successfully completing elementary and secondary levels. She showed such an aptitude for science and a love for people, that they encouraged her to take nurse's training. She completed this medical training with flying colors, standing at the head of her class upon graduation. Today she is happily married to a Christian businessman and continues to serve as head nurse at the Good Samaritan Hospital.

FRIENDSHIP AND DIALOGUE ARE ESSENTIAL TO THE CHILD'S PERSONHOOD

As we stated in chapter one, a child becomes a person through dialogue. Prior to that important I-Thou relationship he was simply an individual. In *The Meaning of Persons* Paul Tournier tells of his early childhood, "submerged," as he puts it, "in my 'orphan complex.' " He was fearful in those infant years to tell his innermost secrets to persons. Thus he maintained his "friendship" with a little dog who was vital to him. He felt he could only open his deepest thoughts to the animal without fear of criticism. But unfortunately he had chosen a "friend" that could not reply. "The choice was there," he says, "but there was no dialogue," for there was no chance of opposition.

Only as a growing child partakes of responsible dialogue while adhering to his own strongly held opinions can he relate in this fashion. At the same time he always runs that all-important risk of denial.

In all of this, it becomes evident that the child must have learned to accept himself with full conviction. And it is also clear that he must have learned to trust in others. This can only be learned in a Nazareth-like home where the child has been loved, encouraged, "discipled," and allowed to be his own person—and God's.

Dr. Dubois, the great nineteenth-century psychiatrist, made a statement that is not only good for doctors but for parents as well, "Hold out your hand to him . . . Do not be afraid of frankly admitting to him your weaknesses, your inborn shortcomings. Bring yourself close to him . . . ." It is the same interpersonal principle that the Bible uses with reference to THE Person—"Draw near to God and he will draw near to you." Yet God and the parent (if he is faithful) will continually encourage the child in his personal integrity and individuality.

Sir Edmund Gosse relates how he first became aware that he was a person quite distinct from his parents. It occurred on the day that he realized he knew something his father did not. "The theory that my father was omniscient or infallible was now quite dead and buried . . . . There was a secret in this world and it belonged to me!"

It is this mutuality of understanding, forbearance, and communication that Roy Croft undoubtedly had at the turn of the century when he wrote:

I love you, not only for what you are
But for what I am when I am with you.
I love you, not only for what
You have made of yourself
But what you are making of me.

I love you for the part of me that you bring out
I love you for putting your hand
Into my heaped up heart and passing over
All the foolish, weak things
That you can't help seeing there,
And for drawing into the light
All the beautiful belongings
That no one else had looked quite far enough to find.

I love you because you are helping me to make
Out of the lumber of my life
Not a tavern, but a temple;
Out of the works of my every day
Not a reproach but a song.

You have done it without a touch
Without a word, without a sign.
You have done it by being yourself.
Perhaps that is what being a friend means
After all.

Making friends with people from every background is a God-designed craft that our children will follow when it grows out of the warmth of our family life.

And having learned to make friends, to relate freely and without reservation, a child can feel free to understand. The walls are broken down and he can relax with his parents as they lead him into a learning experience that will broaden his horizons. In the following pages we shall examine together ways in which a boy or girl, surrounded by love, can be strongly motivated to learn vital skills, attitudes, and concepts.

NINE
HELPING HIM IN LEARNING

Almost every parent can remember that first day in school
when he himself was a child. It was either a painful experience,
or joyful, depending on the teacher. Most of us can probably
count on one hand the teachers whom we considered *really*
good. I remember a Miss Hall in my first grade. I thought she
was beautiful—a warm, responding person whom all her pupils
loved. I can also envision Mrs. Smith, my sixth-grade teacher.
She too loved her children—all of them. And how they
reacted! I can to this day recall meaningful data that I learned
in their classes—not because it was learned by rote, but
because it was surrounded by excitement, drama, *and love*.

Unfortunately, there are always teachers that actually *dislike*
children—*all* children. To them teaching is just a chore.
Concerning these, Gilbert Highet in *The Art of Teaching* has
said, "If any teacher finds himself disliking *all* his pupils, he
should change his character, and if that fails, change his job!"

Of course, there are always those schools and children
that, on first acquaintance, are not very lovable or even likable.
This has always been true. There are some neighborhoods
where youngsters have been turned into little demons by their
environment and their homes. Some schools are sloughs of
despond! Charles Dickens in *Nicholas Nickelby* describes a
school of nineteenth-century England in his picture of

Dotheboys Hall where children terrorized their headmaster and his family. The history of the American frontier is replete with tales of bullies that beat and drove away long successions of teachers. The question, however, remains: Do we leave it at that, or do we provide relevance to a solid learning regimen? Can we transform the child's natural instinct for reluctance to learning into a positive excitement?

Often racial differences—a white teacher with black students—or a Chicano teacher with white pupils—point up the resistance. Yet this, too, can be overcome (as demonstrated by the movies *To Sir, with Love* and *Conrack*), with the understanding heart.

RULES FOR TEACHING

Manifestly, there are basic rules for teaching, and children do not learn without them. They are simple and to the point:

1. *The teacher must know his subject.* This sounds like a cliché but it is not. Our schools are loaded with teachers who are not immersed in their subject matter. There are French teachers who stumble over anything harder than the Third Reader. There are chemistry teachers who are just a jump ahead of their classes. And there are English teachers who do not speak the king's English (or the queen's).

2. *The teacher must like his subject!* There are too many teachers caught in the treadmill of subjects that bore them, and they drone through them while their students sleep, or play. I had a science teacher who had been a pastor and who had been assigned the task of teaching biology. He hated it, and so did his students. More especially, we did not like him because he pretended an enthusiasm he did not possess. Highet remarks about such teachers: "The young dislike their elders for having fixed minds. But they dislike them even more for being insincere!"

3. *The teacher must love his students.* If not, as we have mentioned above, he should abandon teaching. He should mix

with them informally on occasion. He might invite them (in small groups) to his home for parties. He should invent learning games for them in class. The key word for the teacher is "listen"; hear with the "third ear" what youngsters are saying to one another, to him, and to their world. From time to time, he should put aside his notes and simply talk to them from his heart, out of his experiences. Children will love him for it.

I have mentioned these major points to indicate where I think we may be failing in our schools (and homes) as we try to encourage youngsters along the path of learning.

TEACHING READING

Parents have often complained to me that their children do not love reading. Joan Enoch, a reading specialist, has suggested some methods whereby a child may be encouraged to read. Since reading is the *sine qua non* of all future learning, I am listing hers and others below:

1. Employ a vital and stimulating vocabulary in your child's presence. He will listen and learn meanings of words, often without looking them up, simply by hearing the context. When a child asks, "What does that word mean?" of course, a simple definition will be sufficient.

2. Provide various exciting vocabulary games to be played by the whole family in the evenings. Games such as *Scrabble, Go to the Head of the Class,* etc., are not only fun but tremendously enriching. Reading games and Bible drill are exciting and too often neglected in our television era.

3. Encourage the child to follow sermons in the Bible, to use the hymnbooks. On a more mundane level, let him read the menu in the restaurant and help order the meals.

4. Provide a wealth of good reading material on your bookshelves. Sets of reference books, encyclopedias, although expensive, are worth their weight in gold. "Pour your money into your mind and no one can steal it from you," a wise man once said. Volumes of classics, subscriptions to news

magazines, good children's periodicals all enhance a child's reading ability *if* they are read and used by the *whole* family. Encourage the child, when he asks a question, to run and look it up in the *World Book* or *Britannica Junior* (or others).

5. Encourage children to watch the better programs on educational television. Help them choose the right viewings by referring regularly to a TV listing and watching for those that are not only exciting but elevating.

6. Be sure that you are doing continual reading yourself— reading of all varieties—news, sports, classics, magazines, science fiction, or whatever. A child that sees his parents reading and enjoying books will catch the "disease." Use the public library and family reference books, and involve your youngster in planning real and imaginary trips. Outline such "trips" using an atlas, road-map, and magazines such as *National Geographic*.

7. When the child is small, it is good to read to him regularly. Tests have shown that a preschool child will learn to read more easily in direct proportion to the times he has had stories read to him in his preliterate days. He learns to point out pictures and large words, he watches the eye motion of his parent (from left to right in the Western world) and picks up the skill with remarkable ease.

8. When on business trips, at home or overseas, collect stamps, coins and postcards for the child on your return. Gathering interesting menus, brochures of foreign lands, airplane tickets, airline magazines is fascinating to a child, whetting his appetite for greater knowledge.

9. Encourage your child to read to you things that interest him. When he says, "Listen to this, Mom," take a moment to display real enthusiasm.

10. Asking your youngster questions about what she has read motivates the child to greater achievement. "What did you like best about [J. R. R. Tolkien's] *The Hobbit*?" or "What did Thing One and Thing Two do in [Dr. Seuss'] *The Cat in the Hat*?" are sample questions that stimulate the child.

11. Encouraging your child's self-image by praising his achievements in activities that relate to his reading, such as spelling, vocabulary building, etc., will recharge his

enthusiasm. Such reinforcement requires little time but yields great dividends.

Children that come from homes with such encouragement display high achievement in their school experience. Alan Button in *The Authentic Child* says, "If you see these parents and their children alone at home, interacting with each other in mutual love and respect, you see that they subscribe not to the clichés, but [are] strengthened in their togetherness." And, he adds, "You understand why the youngsters are so shining and so effective in school."

We have found that even the surrogate home will often provide this accepting environment within which learning can proceed successfully. Dong Min Children's Home in Korea was just such a setting a quarter of a century ago. Sam Yang wrote to me of his boyhood experience: "My mother died of tuberculosis when I was in third grade, but my father struggled on, caring for me and my two brothers while going to work daily. Then suddenly three months later, he was killed in a traffic accident. He had been a professor in a nearby Christian college and had taught us all to love literature. I constantly had a book in my hand.

"After his death, we were desperate, as I was the oldest and we had no means of support. In a few days the mayor of our town learned of our plight and made arrangements for us to be received into Dong Min Orphanage in Mokpo City. It was a strange 'birthday' for me and my brothers when we entered the home on March 2, 1962. I remember that it was a cold, wet day and we felt so forlorn.

"At first the life of an orphanage seemed unbearable to us, because we were so used to Father's and Mother's closeness to us. But the housemothers loved us almost as much as if we had been their own children, and the superintendent became like a new father to us. Thankfully, they had provided a good basic library at the home, and my brothers and I continued with our reading.

"In three years I graduated from primary school and had become somewhat of a father to my young brothers. They mourned so deeply for our parents, and I often heard them crying in their beds at night.

"After graduation the superintendent encouraged me to go

to middle school because I had done so well in my studies. It was not easy, for the new school was six kilometer's distance, and I had to walk both ways. There was no bus in those days. But I was determined to attend and went daily, rain or shine and even in the heavy winters."

(The superintendent added his note to say how he had encouraged Sam to continue. "His reading and writing made us very proud, and we knew he would succeed if he persevered . . . .")

"In time I finished high school with God's help, and prayed that I might have the opportunity to enter Mokpo Teachers' College. But they gave a stiff entrance examination, and the other applicants seemed so brilliant.

"I remember praying at that time, 'Lord, if you open the door, I will study harder than ever so that I can teach and lead children to you.' God answered. Besides scoring high in the exams, I received a scholarship. After that, he prepared me through my reading and curriculum.

"If I were to credit anyone with success, it would be my superintendent who loved the Bible. He lived so close to God that I felt his warmth. When I graduated at twenty-one, he opened the way for my teaching career."

Dr. Tournier, on talking about the importance that God's presence and his Word have on our lives, concludes that this is a lifelong dialogue:

"When the Word of God strikes a man . . . he perceives that God has been speaking to him for a long time."

This is a phenomenon that many people have commented upon. Augustine at the time of his conversion in Milan, looked back and recalled how often God had spoken to him before: "Thou wert with me, Lord, but I was not with Thee."

"The dialogue was already going on in the darkness of the unconscious before it broke out into the full light of day," adds Tournier.

BUILDING A STORE OF WORDS
Growing out of a child's reading schedule is the natural development of his vocabulary. What he hears from his

parents and what he sees in books as a child are responsible for his word usage in later life. Dr. Paul Diederich of Educational Testing Service reports that children read more books at eight than at any other period of life. This is likely the reason for his word-supply growth at that time. Between eight and ten, the studies reveal, he acquires nearly 70 percent of his grown-up vocabulary. An additional 25 percent accumulates between ten and twenty-five. Only 5 percent is added after that age.

If he is ever to love reading, age eight will be the time when he gobbles books wholesale. I have watched library reading rooms and observed that the children's section has the highest representation from this age-level.

Children dote on new words at this age. I still visualize my nephew's love affair with his dictionary when he was nine. He gloated over each word-gem as though it were gold. As a result he scored high on aptitude and intelligence tests at each level. Lewis Terman, author of the Stanford-Binet IQ tests, said, "Vocabulary is the best single indicator of intelligence in our culture."

It is the common coin of our cultural realm. It assists the young person as he lands his first position. It is a bridge into a successful university career. It oils the interpersonal machinery as he deals with other students or colleagues. It enriches the person's life inwardly and outwardly. It helps his intellect grow even further. It opens gates to wider endeavors.

On the other hand, a lack of rich vocabulary can seriously hamper both child and adult. Dr. A. Broyard in his *Children of the Counterculture* says, "An anemic vocabulary can be even more damaging than an unhealthy diet."

A child needs to begin honing and polishing words as soon as he can speak. A parent can help him in a purposeful way to widen his word potential on a regular basis. There are so many ways to do it—the dictionary is vital. But I have watched parents use flash cards, scrap books, pictures, and drawing as levers for word-growth. It is said of Wilfred Funk, who with Wagnall created a dictionary, that he always wrote down words he wanted to recall. He wrote them down in a special notebook and committed them to memory. My own device as a young person was a tiny pocket diary. I determined that I would add three words a day to my store and would use

at least six times. I am sure I was a trial to my family
and friends. But it was a joy to see my treasure grow.

I can recall the particular enjoyment of word-studies. To
learn that the word "steward" derived from two old English
words: "sty" and "warden"; "a person who cares for pigs,"
was a revelation to me. And from this also developed the name
"Stewart," the title of one of the great Scottish royal dynasties.
Or there was the word, "sheriff," originating from two English
words: "shire" and "reeve"; the authority in charge of a shire.

A parent who loves words can engender in his youngster a
love for the sound and shape of words. The look-up system
can become a lifelong game for a person beginning in his
childhood. The habit of referring to the dictionary is hard to
break, once established.

Reading to the youngster is an important link in word-building.
"It is easy to pick out the child to whom his parents have
read," a teacher told me not long ago. "He has the largest
word-supply of any of my pupils."

Stories read to a child can be stories lived. Anyone who has
read "Goldilocks" to a four-year-old knows the joy of
dramatizing the parts: heroine, daddy bear, mother bear, and
baby bear. The child is spellbound. The adult outdoes
himself because of his attentive audience—often "hamming" it
beyond belief. The child literally enters the story, often
acting it out. Bible stories can be enjoyed in the same way.
Children participate in the emotion of the story: crying,
laughing, chanting—but most of all, being spellbound.

I remember my mother reading *Treasure Island* to my
ten-year-old brother while he was sick in bed. When her voice
became hoarse and she had to quit, he impatiently grabbed
the book and finished it himself. It was then that he discovered
that reading was fun.

Make a record of new words. The little pocket diary of
accumulating words worked well for me. I have seen others use
a card file. Expose him to good growth books that will stretch
his abilities a bit. Reading "imprints" in him new words far
better than do movies or TV. When we write, print a word, or
repeat a word several times, it becomes ours. Dr. William
Wiener of the New York City College system has done much

research on the effect of children's drawings on later reading
and vocabulary abilities. There is a direct relationship between
early encouragement to draw and print and later literary
aptitude.

Keep defining new words for the child so that he understands
the meaning of what he is saying. I heard one youngster,
an eight-year-old, say, "Well, *financially*, I'd like to do that!"
It soon became clear that he had confused the word
"financially" with "confidentially." A gentle redefinition for
him was in order along with right usage, in two or three
different ways, to set him on the right path. "*Confidentially*,
we can trust him. So we have *confidence* in him because
he keeps *confidential* secrets to himself."

A father, for instance, can help a child understand names
and functions of carpentry tools and lead him to understand
basic English. "This," said one dad, "is a *mitre* box. We use
this to fit the corners of our carpentry together. You see here
how we *mitre* the angles of this door together with it?" He
illustrates as he talks by working steadily and helps his son
to do it for himself, encouraging the youngster to use the word
"mitre" as he saws.

A mother may talk to her daughter about sewing a new
dress. "See," she may say to the child, "this is the way you
baste. Basting often comes first before you put in the permanent
stitches. Let me see you baste this hem, now." Hereby the
mother has used the word "baste" in a variety of settings and
the child is encouraged to use it herself. It soon becomes
a part of her permanent storehouse of terms.

Enjoy word games together. Scrabble has already been
mentioned. But "hangman" is a lot of fun and has been enjoyed
by children of many generations. Instruction on how words
are put together often intrigues a child, especially new scientific
words. Words with mellifluous, important-sounding syllables
usually fascinate. One three-year-old girl learned the word,
"peumonoultramicroscopicsilicovolcanonosis" from her
daddy, and used it to the entertainment—and finally despair
—of her parents. She could spell it both forward and backward.
Needless to say, her IQ was quite high. But children do not

have to learn such high-powered words. A word like *fantastic*
can be broken down into its basic relation to the word *fantasy*
and even understood in its use in Disneyland.

The monthly column on new words in the *Readers Digest* is
helpful to both adults and children and is a good way to
play family games and quiz one another. Your local bookstore
or toy store can probably also suggest word games in addition
to *Scrabble*.

Our overseas children have a built-in method of learning
new words through writing letters to their sponsors in countries
overseas. Children in normal families can enjoy word usage
by writing letters to Grandma or Uncle Ned. Keeping a diary is
another fun way to learn the art of daily scribbling.

It is good to take out the little pocket notebook from time
to time and review the words that were jotted down a month
ago. As in everything else, recapitulation is an ideal way
of affirming a half-forgotten term.

OTHER HELPS

Helping the schools can be done by any parent. Surveys
universally attest to the fact that the *first reason* for trouble
in the schools is a discipline deficiency in the home. Discipline
in our definition, as noted previously, means "discipling or
helping the child control himself." Too often parents defend
their children in cases of schoolroom misconduct. Often
grownups have some unresolved hostilities against schools
stemming from their own childhood. "Don't listen to that d--n
teacher!" a parent may tell his child. There is no faster
way to undermine respect for authority or teacher competence
than this negative reinforcement from the home. A Christian
home will want to encourage a child's cooperation and
(whenever possible) even love for the teacher.

Disrepect also for others' rights is a common cause of trouble
in the classroom. Vandalism is costing the taxpayer millions
of dollars. In too many neighborhoods, respect for public or
private property is virtually nonexistent. Damaged windows,
furniture, and walls are a common sight in many schools. Petty

theft has reached epidemic proportions—theft of books, pencils, typewriters, personal belongings, and innumerable other items are stolen daily. "They owe it to you," is the attitude usually expressed. Inbred values and morals develop from babyhood in the home.

Studying model schools helps. Dr. William Glasser, author of *Schools Without Failure,* has worked for years in centers for delinquent and pre-delinquent children in Santa Monica, California. We have referred briefly to his work in earlier pages. It is his contention that his children need to assume a success-identity before they can perform effectively either in school or elsewhere. He has some basic principles that are helpful even for parents with fairly well-adjusted children. His points can assist a parent with his child:

1. *Children who fail, revert to emotion* to guide their behavior. *Successes can depend on logic and reason.*

2. The child must be encouraged to *make a value judgment on the reasons* for his failure.

3. *No one should attempt to change the world* in order for the child to succeed. A child should be allowed to suffer from results of his behavior.

4. The parent and teacher *remain personal and warm* to the child and do not rehearse his failures to him. They indicate, nevertheless, that they *expect success.*

5. The child is *responsible to make a choice* on the right course for his own success.

6. The *child should commit himself* to this course of action.

7. Finally, Dr. Glasser cites what he considers the keystone to his "reality therapy": *Once the child has made his choice and committed himself to a course of action, no excuse is accepted for not pursuing it.*

Helen Keller is an example cited to illustrate this. Annie Sullivan accepted no emotional excuse for Helen's failure to follow through, regardless of her many handicaps. Success remained the goal always. Result: Helen succeeded!

HELP MAKE TEACHING RELEVANT

This is not always possible, as in teaching a mathematical formula or, perhaps, $E = MC^2$. But in most instances, subjects can be made most relevant to a child's life. This is especially true of Bible teaching, both in Sunday school and out.

Often a teacher will ask her class, "Does reading have any meaning for you outside of school?" Sometimes as many as 75 percent will answer "no" or "except for the sports page and the comics."

Studies show that only 10 percent of the children are truly dedicated readers. When asked, "Suppose I should give you ten dollars to buy a book. What would you get?" children are usually stymied. Very few youngsters in the sixth grade have ever been in a bookstore. Far fewer—perhaps three—out of a class of fifty, have ever purchased a book. "What does your father or mother read?" was the next question. The average reply was "the daily paper." When asked about schoolbooks and their relationship to daily life, there was genuine puzzlement. School books are for school life—nothing else, according to the great majority. Only those few who saw a true relationship could be considered successful students. *Without relevance to life, lessons lack motivation to learn.*

My wife and I still treasure a church school essay written by our youngest daughter when she was six. The teacher encouraged her to write what came into her mind and not to worry about spelling or punctuation. The following was her brief essay:

GOD LOVES YOU AND LOVES YOUR FAINDS [friends].

GOD WILL HLAP YOU IN YOU'R SLOOG [school]

AND PLAY TOO.

GOD WILL HLAP YOU IN ANY THAING.

GOD LOVE'S BOYS.

YES GOD LOVE'S BOY'S.

GOD LOVES ANY THAING.

THE BURAD'S AND THE DOG'S

AND MAWST ANY THAING.

IN JESUS NAME a MEN.

Her doctrine, spelling, and sentence structure were faulty. But we are glad she saw a relationship between her life and God's even at that tender age. Encouraging children to write and draw what they feel and think as they react to lesson material is one of the quickest ways to establish relevance in learning.

According to Dr. Gilbert Highet (*The Art of Teaching*), the teacher has two special functions:

One: "*To make a bridge between school and the world.*" And the best way for a teacher to do this (i.e., make the subject relevant) is "to *make himself relevant.*" He illustrates this with a slight but forgivable exaggeration. "Nine thousand times more pupils have learnt a subject well because *they felt the teacher's vitality* than because of the subject for its own sake."

The second function for a teacher is to "*make a bridge between youth and maturity.*" It is the job of the teacher (and the parent) to make adulthood understandable to childhood.

The great Adams family, producer of two presidents of the United States, has had a continuing effect throughout history. This was largely due to the ability of this dynasty to teach and be taught. In *The Education of Henry Adams* the autobiographer tells what swayed his future. "A teacher," he says, "affects eternity; he can never tell where his influence stops!"

One of the children who grew up in Europe during the aftermath of World War Two was Johann Meiner. He was born in Bavaria, Germany, in 1942, and survived a babyhood troubled with the sound of shells and confusion. Due to pressures of war, his parents separated when he was only three and he was abandoned. Admitted to one of the homes that Christian Children's Fund was helping, he was placed in a cottage with a brilliant, motherly houseparent who accepted him immediately. Her songs and stories began to have an influence on him almost at once. He soon evidenced great

verbal ability even at ages four and five. His gift for verse
writing was especially apparent during his high school years,
when he produced some poetry of great sensitivity.

After graduation he became an editor on the Munich Merkur,
a well-known Bavarian journal. In late 1967 he published
a volume of poems that were an immediate success. This
led to a lecture tour throughout Europe, highlighted by a
presentation of his work at the University of Warsaw. Yet,
despite his success, he recognizes its origins. Recently Johann
wrote to his old housemother in Munich, "My home and my
heart are still there with you!"

A study made of graduates of homes and schools affiliated
with various child-care agencies indicates their surprising
success. One of the basic reasons was attributed to the warm
home setting the children experienced. The other was the
stress laid upon reading and verbal skills. The survey indicated
that 49 percent had gone into some form of professional
activity such as art, teaching, religion, business, medicine, or
law. The balance were shown by this after-care analysis to
have entered some form of skilled activity. Many of the girls
had married and established fine Christian homes. Five percent
of them had chosen to remain in children's work, becoming
housemothers or superintendents in orphanages of India,
Africa, and Latin America. It was interesting also to note that at
least a quarter of the children entered a people-related
vocation in later life: 14 percent becoming nurses, 10 percent
teachers, 5 percent church-related professions, and 1 percent
physicians—or nearly one-third directly serving the needs of
others through their occupation. Add to that Christian mothers
and fathers (probably 90 percent of the whole) and the
orphanage housemothers mentioned above, and we readily see
the importance of warm, accepting, success-oriented homes.

One prestigious graduate came from an affiliated orphan
school named Dr. Graham's Homes, high in the Himalaya
mountains. The superintendent of this beautiful institution
wrote:

"One of our most successful 'old boys' is Commodore George
Douglas, DSO (Retd.) of the Indian Navy. After leaving our
home, he went to sea, joining the Navy as an able-bodied
seaman. A few years later he became an air pilot and won

various decorations for valor during combat operations. In one of them he was quite badly wounded. Eventually he became head of the Indian Fleet's Air Arm which was based on the Vikrant, an Indian aircraft carrier. Having distinguished himself in many service activities, he was honorably retired and now resides in Canada."

Another superintendent wrote gratefully regarding the influence of one of her graduates who is now serving in the State of Orissa, populated by 60 million people and having only one 200-bed hospital:

"Jakob is one of our fine Christian boys who worked hard to become a doctor. Now he is serving in this region where there are no other doctors or nurses for miles around. In his late twenties, Jakob has become greatly beloved, for God seems to have given him a great gift as a medical healer."

It seems clear that teachers and parents can do more through enthusiasm and emotional content (plus excellence) than any other influence on our children. Johann Von Goethe said concerning one of his own teachers:

"Such a teacher who can arouse a feeling for one single good action, for one single good poem, accomplishes more than he who fills our memory with rows on rows of natural objects, classified with name and form."

In a chapter on this subject years ago I wrote a summary for parents. The principles seem still valid:

1. Remember that failures in schoolwork are not so important as the well-being of the child. If he is doing maximum work, he should be praised, not scolded. "Did you do your best?" should be the criterion.

2. Keep uppermost the child's hopes and dreams for himself—not your dreams for him.

3. Grades on a report card should stimulate the child, not inhibit him. If report cards are defeating him, some other type of measure ought to be employed to encourage his efforts.

4. Long and tedious homework should be discouraged. A child's health and growth come first.

5. Pushing a child to develop or learn faster than his natural ability can damage rather than encourage.

6. Infinite patience with the child in his learning process is essential. Scolding and punishment will only rattle, unnerve or frustrate him.

Learning continues throughout a lifetime. But initial steps should be ones chosen carefully by both parent and child. An unknown author has written "What is a Boy?" I have taken the liberty of changing the subject to both "boys and girls" —since both are learners in our homes:

What are Children?
They are persons who are going to carry on what you have started.

He and she sit right where you are sitting and attend when you are gone.

You may adopt all the policies you please, but how they will be carried out depends upon him or her.

Even if you make leagues and treaties, they will have to manage them.

They are going to sit at your desk in the Senate, and occupy your place on the Supreme Bench.

They will assume control of your cities, states, and nation.

They are going to move in, take over your prisons, churches, universities, schools, and corporations.

All your work is going to be judged and praised or condemned by them.

Your reputation and your future are in their hands.

All your work is done for them, and the fate of the nation and of humanity is in their hands—and God's.

So it will be well to pay your children much attention.

Having considered the mental and emotional development of the child, we should go one step deeper—his spiritual development. The final chapter attempts to explore modes and methods that can help him grow closer to God.

TEN
HELPING HIM SPIRITUALLY

The Los Angeles Times recently carried a poignant report on childhood suicides. The thought that despair has brought young lives to this extremity seems hard to comprehend.

"An eleven-year-old," they reported, "had slashed his wrists."

" 'I want to go to heaven,' he sobbed. 'I can't stand these stomach aches and being unhappy . . . . If I could only die . . . it's hard to live . . . living is horrible. I just want to die because nobody cares if I die, so I just want to die!' "

Living a loveless life looks impossible to these youngsters. Other attempted suicides are reporting and follow similar patterns and causes:

A twelve-year-old girl hung her blond-tressed doll by the neck. She then drugged her younger sister and slashed the tot's legs with a pair of scissors. Finally, she slashed her own wrists and took an overdose of drugs. "I'd be better off dead," she said when resuscitated. "Then no one will need to look at my ugly face anymore!"

A five-year-old girl became obsessed with kitchen knives. She then burned her three-year-old sister with matches and attempted choking her with a shoestring. When nothing else worked she climbed out the window and ran out into heavy traffic, inviting a speedy death.

A sadly successful suicide was reported concerning a six-year-old boy who said, "I want to die because no one loves me." Then he attempted to cut himself with his father's razor. Later that day he was discovered hanging from a second-floor window by a sashcord.

Only recently have authorities realized that a child can feel such depths of inner pain. Howard Clinebell in *The Intimate Marriage* calls this a "need for a sense of at-homeness in the universe." When unmet the child is alone in a cosmos lacking what Erikson terms "basic trust." The need has been noted through the ages and unless our homes and lives supply this, the child has an unquenchable sense of disquiet. Ultimately, of course, his need will be met only in a redeeming Lord.

"Thou hast made us for Thyself, O Lord," said Augustine, "and our hearts are ever restless until they find their rest in Thee." There is, according to Pascal's *Pensees*, a "God-shaped vacuum in every human heart." The drive to relate to the loving Spirit of God is an unavoidable dimension in a child's drive for deeper community.

When a six-year-old says, "I want to die because nobody loves me," he is expressing not only a lack of human relationships but a universal hunger for God. The most frequent cause for such a child's ultimate dejection is the emotional poverty he finds in his home. Often, too, such a child has known a suicide in his own family, indicating a home pattern of disunity and despair.

For many families, according to Morris J. Paulson at UCLA, "the most frequent immediate event . . . is 'abandonment' by a parent figure. For some families, divorce is the ultimate separation of a hostile, feuding, pathological relationship of violence between husband and wife."

BEGIN AT THE BEGINNING
WITH A PERSONAL RELATIONSHIP TO CHRIST

One young couple found themselves at loggerheads and came to me for guidance. They had two small children and were concerned over things the children were seeing and hearing in their quarrels. With the pressure of raising a family and maintaining a business, they were devoting less and less time to one another. Although they had both at one time professed a love for Christ, it was hidden now under layers of hostility. Eventually I suggested a trial period of one month in which they faithfully observed a family devotions hour. "Speak to the Lord as simply as you are speaking to me," I urged them. "Tell him the depths of your need, and your children's. Name them by name in your prayer. Eventually you will again experience what Scripture calls 'knowing God.' And it is only when a child hears sincerity and meaning that he can relate to the same Lord."

Only when parents have a personal love for God in Christ and regard him as the unique Savior will they be satisfied when children experience a like devotion. The best place for a child to commit his life to Jesus Christ is in the family circle with a mother and father to lead and encourage.

"Give your hearts," said one Christian, "not only into each other's keeping. But place them into the hand of Christ who alone can contain your heart." As the child matures, his sense of unity in life will require an intelligible cohesiveness. As Christians we believe that this is the only unifying philosophy of existence that can satisfy.

Dr. Ray Ortlund (in *Lord, Make My Life a Miracle*) points out, "Many Christians find life is lopsided. Their lives are the wheel, but with too much attention given to the circumference. They are dependent on those who are outside of them, instead of God who is that 'Holy Within.' He must be the hub, the focus, the purpose!"

One of my Japanese friends told me his boyhood dilemma, how he was faced with meaninglessness and chaos after the war. He had grown up in Japan during the twenties and thirties, and life was difficult even then. His father was a Shintoist and a descendant of a Shinto priest. His mother was a devout Buddhist. Like many in that land, it was a strict Japanese family in which the father was the unquestioned head—in every detail. When the worldwide depression of the thirties hit Japan, as it did most other nations, Michi's famly suffered financial reverses. The household savings dwindled to nothing and unemployment spread alarmingly. Michi's father stiffly told his son, "Sorry my son, but we cannot afford to send you to high school. You will have to get a menial job somewhere."

The blow to Michi's pride and security were too great. His inner world had collapsed. That evening his parents found him prone on his bedroom "tatami." His face was a deadly white, his breathing shallow. In alarm, they called Michi's uncle, a physician. The diagnosis: attempted suicide. Rushing him to the hospital, they barely saved his life.

"When I awoke," Michi told me years later, "I seemed to be in the midst of a bright haze. Almost audibly, I heard a voice saying, 'Your life has a purpose, Michi. Find it!' I had no way of knowing which way to turn for such a purpose. Later, however, as I walked down Tokyo's Ginza, I heard singing from a Christian church. In curiosity I entered and sat near the back. As the minister spoke, I felt peculiarly drawn by the voice of One who said, 'Follow me.' And I have followed him ever since."

In his *Markings,* Dag Hammarskjold tells of his conversion experience in these eloquent words, "To let go of the image which, in the eyes of the world, bears your name, the image in your consciousness of social ambition and sheer force of will. To let go and fall—in trust and blind devotion. Toward another, another . . . to take the risk."

A solid marriage is bound together by the rebirth experience. Life overflows when a family experiences this. "My purpose," the Lord said in John's Gospel, "is to give life in all its fullness." Erich Fromm, as a psychiatrist, attests to rebirth from a psychological standpoint, "The aim of life is to be fully born, though its tragedy is that most of us die before we are thus born . . . the answer is . . . to develop one's awareness, one's reason, one's capacity to love, to such a point that one transcends one's own egocentric involvement and arises at a new harmony . . . ." (quoted in Howard Clinebell's *The Intimate Marriage*).

A Christian knows, of course, that this rebirth comes about through the entrance of the living Lord into his life. At that moment of entry, the rest of the world becomes as nothing. Conversation with him is everything. All sham and pretense drop away, for Christ goes straight to the real you. And it is this vital experience we share with our child, in order that he may have life and meaning.

FROM REBIRTH GROW
PERSONAL AND FAMILY DEVOTIONS

No family can afford to be without at least a simple, informal family altar. Certainly grace at table is an essential element that binds a family.

One of the warmest times of togetherness for our overseas homes is that moment of prayer. When even the tiniest member lisps to God the problems of "brother" or "sister," all hostilities cease. This is equally true of all aspects of family altar—grace at meals, song time, evening prayers, and Scripture reading.

It is likely, however, that personal devotions should come first for each member of the family. It is at that moment, perhaps early in the morning, when souls are refreshed before a day's activities.

I have been greatly helped in recent years by the writings of Thomas Kelly, a Quaker from Philadelphia, who taught at Haverford College in the early forties.

"Deep within us all," he writes in *A Testament of Devotion*, "there is an amazing inner sanctuary of the soul, a holy place, a Divine Center, a speaking Voice, to which we may continuously return . . . . It is a Light Within, which illumines the face of God and casts new shadows and new glories upon the face of men . . . . It is the Shekinah of the soul, the Presence in the midst."

Often our problem is the problem of Martha of Bethany. We are "busy with many things." "We love Christ," says Ortlund, "but we don't stay much around him!"

That hour (or half hour) in the morning can light up the day for us. I find my day is usually tasteless without it. When I remember it is filled with adventure and expectancy. "It is a wonderful discovery to find that you are a temple, that you have a church inside of you, there God is. In hushed silence, attend to Him. 'The Lord is in His holy temple!' " said George Fox.

Scripture is clear on the subject: "In thy presence is fulness

of joy; at thy right hand there are pleasures for evermore . . . .
My presence shall go with thee and I will give thee rest"
(Psalm 16:11; Exodus 33:14).

FAMILY DEVOTIONS COME NEXT

Jack Taylor in his fine book, *One Family Under God,* suggests
some steps for setting up and maintaining a family devotion
time. They are:

1. Be convinced in your heart that you vitally need a family
altar.

2. Get the family together and let them discuss their need for it.

3. Reach a unanimity as to time and place for it.

4. Start having it at once.

He then suggests ways for planning the agenda of such a family
altar:

1. Let it be short.

2. Let it be scriptural.

3. Get the whole family involved.

4. Don't let it slide into sermons or scoldings.

5. Keep it informal but not frivolous.

6. Make it interesting, removing dullness and doing creative
things.

7. *Try variety at the family altar.*

I have watched with excitement as our homes around the world
have experimented with fresh approaches to devotional times.
I can still hear the clear young voices of Korean children
singing "How Great Thou Art" (in their own language) in early
morning mists on Nam San hilltop outside the city of Seoul.
In India, I have watched a group of youngsters in Madras
acting out a Bible story in song on a moonlit beach overlooking
the Bay of Bengal. I have visited with children at morning
devotions in camps in the Philippines, Taiwan, and Colombia.

Our own family has had its family altar under the trees in the Shenandoah Valley of Virginia. It all brought a fuller appreciation of his presence surrounded as we were by chirping of early-singing birds and slanting sunlight.

Families can use a variety of sources for their inspiration —always fresh, never hackneyed. The Bible with its many fine versions is of course always first. *The Living Bible* is a favorite with children and adults alike because of its vivid idiomatic English. *The New International Bible* is helpful for Bible study due to its scholarly handling of the original manuscripts. *The New English Bible* and *The Good News Bible* are excellent versions to share on different mornings. And it would be a shame to omit the stately and sublime King James Version, particularly in its poetic books such as Psalms and sections of Isaiah.

DON'T NEGLECT MUSIC AT YOUR WORSHIP HOUR

Evangelical songs have changed radically and often beautifully in the past ten years. Christian musicians often distinguish between what they describe as "praise and Scripture" music, and music intended for concert or choir presentations.

Yvonne Alaniz of Costa Mesa's "Maranatha Music" provides simple melodies and memorable words. These choruses are often used in church and Sunday school worship. They are easy for congregations to sing and are intended for participative worship. Most chorus words are simple—often relying on a single Scripture verse: "Seek ye first the kingdom of God, and his righteousness. And all these things shall be added unto you. Allelu, alleluia." Or there is the popular use of a single theme, "God is so good . . . He's so good to me." These are quiet and contemplative choruses that children love.

Use of records at altar time is enjoyed by all. Transcriptions of contemporary gospel music have been popularized by such headliners as Evie Tornquist, B. J. Thomas, Pat and Debbie Boone, and Dave Boyer. This kind of music has universal appeal to all age groups and can add substantially to a time of family worship.

Or some families prefer traditional recordings like those of the Johnny Mann singers or the Gaithers. But whatever the choice, music will add a dimension recommended by the Bible—"come before his presence with singing."

Homemade music with piano, guitar, or harmonica draws a family even closer. Choruses sung *a cappella* should often be used. And traditional hymn books from Sunday school and church draw a family closer to its spiritual roots.

CONTINUAL FELLOWSHIP IS PROBABLY THE MOST IMPORTANT THING

Fellowship begins when the couple is married and continues after the children are born. It is a way of accepting and intuiting one another. The home may be the only place in society where husband, wife, and child are truly heard and heeded. "It is impossible," says Tournier [in *To Understand Each Other*], "to overemphasize the immense need men have to be really listened to, to be taken seriously, to be understood." Here is pollination and birth of living. "No one can develop in this world and find full life without feeling fully understood by at least one person."

The couple and children that hear one another's deep cries, are ones that can fortify each other against life's worst attacks. T. S. Eliot perceives this interdependence when he causes one of his protagonists to say to his mate, "The new person —us!" Gestalt therapy states that identity in marriage occurs when two persons overlap and merge, at least partially. They together become parts of a unified "field."

Years ago when one of my organizations was working in Puerto Rico, I met a family named Ramirez. They were very poor and were being helped by our family assistance program until they could become self-sustaining. I happened by one Saturday when Manuel and his son Juan were planting a small tree in their tiny yard. Unaware of my presence, they were absorbed in their common task. Manuel turned up the dirt with a short pickaxe. Juan removed the loose earth with his small shovel. Carefully they placed the tree into the hole and covered the roots with dirt and compost. I noted how each then touched the trunk of the tree, almost as though in silent blessing. Meanwhile in an open shed nearby were Consuelo, his wife, and their little daughter, Marta, doing the wash. There was a murmur of conversation between them that sounded like mutual appreciation. It is the sort of well-adjusted family one gladly meets from time to time all over the globe. It has no particular connection with economic status, but represents a family group of mutually affirming members. As I visited longer with the Ramirez household, I found that they were also happy members of a local church, enjoying its fellowship and contributing to its strength. Erikson in *Childhood and Society* comments on the necessity of such common undergirding: "The individual ego can be strong only through a mutual guarantee of strength given to and received by all whose life-cycles intertwine."

It is sad to see in our world how uprooting of village and rural life has disturbed the family. "Roots are torn out," says Erikson, "or are brought along, dry up in transit or are kept moist and alive, find an appropriate soil, or fail to take hold and wither." Howard Clinebell adds, "Creative family intimacy is made difficult for many by the anxiety of insulation from the nourishing exchange of community life."

Los Angeles has been described as "300 towns in search of a city." But one of L.A.'s saving graces, I feel, is the multitude of fine churches that help compose its metropolitan sprawl. It has been reliably estimated that there are nearly three million evangelical Christians in the relatively small and concentrated area bounded by L.A. and Orange counties. It is possible that this vital church community contributes to moral and emotional stability for so many uprooted folk from the east.

I have observed the same phenomenon among recently urbanized folk in Seoul, Korea. There despite uprooting from a rural area to the east, the Kim Pak family found fellowship in the church and meaning in one another. Being part of the church subculture has kept alive the interpersonal communication between the Paks and their three children.

We have all known those moments when the "vibes" between two souls are alive. The profound emotion of family ties and memories, especially in moments of crisis, bring members closer than words can ever do.

In *The Meaning of Persons* Tournier tells the story of a woman who related to him some deep moment from her childhood. She spoke slowly and carefully to him as she tried to be completely truthful. "Suddenly," he says, "I found myself trembling inwardly . . . I felt as if I were confronted by something supernatural, something that overwhelmed me."

There are times in the telling of profound facts that the moment "passes from information to communion . . . . Information is intellectual, whereas communion is spiritual." This experience at certain junctures validates every true family. I have found it at my brother's tragic early death, when a hand on a shoulder was enough. I have seen it between husband and wife when their baby was dangerously ill and they hovered above his crib. I felt it deeply in spiritual retreat, when there were nothing but trees overhead and the silence of a Christian family knelt together.

STRESS THAT ALL OF LIFE IS A MINISTRY

The story of Benjamin West, the great American painter, is an intriguing one. It started one day in his childhood when his mother left him alone with his sister Sally. Out of boredom he decided to paint Sally's picture. Searching the kitchen, he found some containers of colored ink, and when his mother unexpectedly returned she found the kitchen in a complete mess. Instead of scolding him, however, she picked up the amateur portrait and remarked, "What do you know. It's Sally!" In reminiscing years later, West remarked, "That day, my mother's kiss made me a painter."

The sequel to the story came about a dozen years later when West was being censured by his Quaker church for performing the worldly skills of an artist. However, when they noticed how devoted he was and how beautiful were his pictures, the elders of his meeting-house gathered together. Laying hands on his head, they prayed, "Lord, this day, we ordain our brother, Benjamin West, to the ministry of painting!"

Fritz Kunkel has stated in his book *In Search of Maturity* that the average home is 40 percent group-oriented and 60 percent ego-oriented. "Children," he says, "and primitive tribes are collective in reactions. Their inner attitude is the original we-feeling." As they mature, adults tend to exchange the group center for the individual center, moving back more toward ego-centeredness. The more they do this, shifting the

ego percentage balance in the family from 40 percent to possibly 80 percent, the more maladjusted they become. As they move toward the 100 percent mark of egocentricity, their actions become increasingly neurotic, noncooperative and anti-Christian. Thus, the maladjusted person needs to become like a child again as Jesus reminded us, "Except you become as a little child you cannot enter the kingdom of God."
In the rebirth experience he discovers anew that the group is his social center, and behind the group must be Christ. The person needs to revert to his childhood without forgetting his adult context and his individual responsibility. From this renewed, reborn we-feeling and his matured individual consciousness arises a creative we-experience of mature Christianity and true ministry.

This new creative center of a person's being should be his positive relationship to the Lord. The person's selfhood should be the experience of his dependence on God, whom he knows only partially but increasingly as he draws closer in his devotional life. A person realizes his real power only when he lives from his real Center—Jesus Christ. Then he can become a channel of creativity and blessing. If he moves away from this new Self and into his own ego, he is cut off from any new power-flow. The modicum power that he does have left causes him anxiety because he has tasted the fullness in his rebirth and true ministry experience.

Robert Browning expressed it in one of his verses,

Faith is my waking life:
One sleeps indeed, and dreams at intervals, we know
But waking to faith is the main point with us!

WITNESSING TO HIS
FAITHFULNESS IS THE PURPOSE OF IT ALL

For families saturated with the love of Christ, there is always an unconscious witness. When neighbors see a tranquil family immersed in love, they watch with eager interest. It is so different from the rest of the world. But we need to look constantly to our personal and household motivation. Thomas Kelly speaking to Christians in Philadelphia forty years ago said, "Do you really want to live your lives, every moment of your lives in His Presence? Do you look for Him, crave Him? Do you love His presence?"

We should never let a day pass without reading our Bible and praying. There can be a tranquility about this experience because we surround ourselves with the love of Christ. "Dark as my path may seem to others," Helen Keller wrote, "I carry a magic light in my heart. Faith, the spiritual strong search-light illumines the way. Although sinister doubts lurk in the shadow, I walk unafraid toward the Enchanted Wood where the foliage is always green . . . ." Helen's friends and neighbors attested to her abiding trust as she traveled, deaf and blind, through life with her hand in his. "I go," she said, "where joy abides, where nightingales nest and sing, and where life and death are one in the presence of my Lord."

Pascal in his *Pensées* comments, "The surest sign of a godless man is that he is afraid to be by himself in a single room, alone."

Children need the constant reminder that God is at the center of all living. Without faith in the Lord, they are deprived of the strongest motivation for good conduct. It is not fair for parents not to share their faith with him and to tell them that they are avoiding wrong and doing right because they love him. Too many parents tell children, "You must not do that because it is socially unacceptable," or "because the neighbors will talk." Morality should be replanted in the reason for it all—God himself.

Several Christian philosophers have spoken of the "cut-flower culture" in which we live. Too many people live in this florist culture in which the flower of morality is about to die. It has been clipped from the original roots that were firmly embedded in the Christian gospel. The only reason for the slight morality we now know seems to be to its social acceptability inherited from a former Christian culture.

Judge George A. Timone of the New York City Court of Domestic Relations in the 1950s listed in the *New York Times* what he thought had to be done to return families to a relatively crimeless society:

The family must teach and live in a belief in the existence of a God who watches and listens.

The home must believe in the dignity of man and the sacredness of life.

The parents must believe and lead their children regarding one's responsibility to the moral law as formulated in the Bible.

They must believe in the basic equality of all men under God who is the Source of the rights of mankind.

They must believe in the protection of such God-given rights as the fundamental purpose of law.

T. S. Eliot called the people of this age, "hollow men . . . stuffed men . . . leaning together . . . headpieces filled with straw . . . ."

As in Abraham's day, godly homes today need to rise above the common run. He prayed, "If there are just ten righteous people in Sodom, Lord, will you spare the city?" Many Christians feel that the church is the salt of the world—a preservative, keeping society from its pell-mell flight toward destruction.

A Christian home can aid its society and a hungry world by joining hunger walks instituted by many denominations. It can have a regular prayer list of missionary and other Christian causes. It can give to the causes of society such as the Red Cross and other drives.

Many households sponsor a foreign child through one of the great children's agencies. I have watched new sponsors as with glowing eyes they choose a case history after I have spoken at churches. These youngsters become very real and very "near" although separated by thousands of miles.

Hope Friedmann told of her experience after she had chosen one child's case history at an organizational banquet. "I did not realize it then," she said, "but we [our family] were about to be blessed by Sandor, a child in the mountains of Latin America." She wrote to the youngster and told him about her family and included a family snapshot. Back came his first letter:

Dear Sponsor:
It feels good to know that someone cares enough for me to help me. I live in a poor house, our hometown has a cold climate and it rains a lot. I send a big hug from your sponsor-child . . . Sandor.

"Someone cares ... poor house ... cold climate," she thought. Now she could pray about specific things. For his birthday, the next time she wrote, she sent five dollars for something he needed most. Again his letter was prompt and moving:

Dear Second Mother:
You don't know how happy I am to have your letter and to know that somebody loves me.

"Tears," she said, "welled up within me." "Dear God," she prayed, "did I mean so much to him? His second mother? Someone who loved him?" She read on in the letter,

As Mother's Day is coming, I wish you many happiness and blessing of our Lord. Thank you for the picture you sent .... Please give my love to the rest of the family. I close with a big hug ... Sandor.

Projects like this can unite a family in mutual love for a far-off child—or missionary—or hungry family in India. It can be our way of ministering and witnessing to the love of Jesus.

These children of the world, yours and mine and millions more, are waiting for love. Only from his Word and his Spirit can we learn the lesson of love. Many of them are blessed with cool white homes and green lawns. But most of the world's children are not. One of the moving accounts written by a missionary doctor, Penelope Key, told of her frustration when so many died in Indochina before she could help:

"Today," she wrote, "there were more than 500 mothers with their sick children, waiting their turn. Some will come again tomorrow, and the next day. I choose 200 to 300 children from among them. The rest are the unchosen ...."

She expresses her inward pain for those neglected tots: "There is agony in this choosing .... When I put up my hand and say 'That child is the last one for the morning,' what am I saying to the child after the last one?" She thinks of the anguish of the mother who has been turned away, "How can I rest—or eat or sleep? How can I choose not to see that child? Why did I choose to stop at the child before that one? If I had chosen to see one more child, that child might be alive today."

It is a spiritual moment for Dr. Key. She says, "I have a prayer I use: 'Lord, don't let me have to go on choosing which child. Lord, send more doctors. Lord, send more cots, more hospitals, more medicine, more milk and food . . . . When can *all* my children be chosen for a new, happy life?"

It is the joy and privilege of every parent to choose a new, happy life for his or her child—through love.

FURTHER READING

Bach, George R., and Deutsch, Ronald M. *Pairing*. New York: Peter H. Wyden, Inc., 1975.

Best-Loved Poems of the American People. Garden City, N.Y.: Garden City Publishing Co., 1936. Poem "Love" by Roy Croft.

Briggs, Dorothy Corkille. *Your Child's Self-Esteem*. New York: Doubleday (Dolphin Books), 1970.

Buber, Martin. *I and Thou*. New York: Charles Scribner's Sons, 1958.

Button, Alan. *The Authentic Child*. New York: Random House, 1969.

Clinebell, Howard. *The Intimate Marriage*. New York: Harper & Row, 1970.

Cronley, Connie. "Blackboard Jungle Updated." *TWA Ambassador*, Sept. 1978, pp. 25, ff. Quotes from Sam Moncur and Jerry Mullins.

Dodson, Fitzhugh. *How to Parent*. Los Angeles: Nash Publishing, 1970.

Ellul, Jacques. *False Presence of the Kingdom*. New York: Alfred A. Knopf, 1968.

Enoch, Joan. "You and Your Child's Reading." *This Issue* magazine, September 1978.

Erikson, Erik. *Childhood & Society*. New York: W. W. Norton, 1964.

Fast, Julius. *Body Language*. Philadelphia: M. Evans & Co., 1970.

Ginott, Haim. *Between Parent and Child*. New York: Macmillan, 1965.

Glasser, William. *Identity Society*. New York: Harper & Row, 1972.

Glasser, William. *Reality Therapy*. New York: Harper & Row, 1963.

Glasser, William. *Schools Without Failure*. New York: Harper & Row, 1969.

Gould, Roger. *Transformations*. New York: Simon & Schuster, 1978.

Hammarskjold, Dag. *Markings*. New York: Alfred A. Knopf, 1964.

Highet, Gilbert. *The Art of Teaching*. New York: Alfred A. Knopf, 1950.

Keller, Helen. *The Story of My Life*. New York: Doubleday, 1954.

Kelly, Thomas. *A Testament of Devotion*. New York: Harper & Row, 1941.

Kesey, Ken. *One Flew Over the Cuckoo's Nest*. New York: Viking, 1962.

Kunkel, Fritz. *In Search of Maturity*. New York: Charles Scribner's Sons, 1949.

May, Rollo. *Love and Will*. New York: W. W. Norton, 1969.

Mayer, Nancy. *The Male Mid-Life Crisis*. New York: Doubleday, 1978.

Menninger, Karl. *The Vital Balance*. New York: The Viking Press, 1964.

Missildine, Hugh. *Your Inner Child of the Past*. New York: Simon and Schuster, 1963.

Ortlund, Raymond C. *Lord, Make My Life a Miracle*. Los Angeles: Regal Books, 1974.

Paton, Frank. *The Triumph of the Gospel in the New Hebrides*. New York: Doran, 1908.

Powell, John. *Why Am I Afraid to Tell You Who I Am?* Niles, Ill.: Argus Communicatons, 1969.

Prather, Hugh. *Notes to Myself*. Lafayette, Cal.: Real People Press, 1971.

Raines, Robert. *Lord, Could You Make It a Little Better?* Waco, Texas: Word, Inc., 1976. Poem on p. 54 used by permission of Word Books, Publisher, Waco, Texas.

Schweitzer, Albert. *On the Edge of the Primeval Forest*. London: A. & C. Black, 1922.

Selye, Hans. *The Stress of Life*. New York: McGraw-Hill, 1956.

Seuss, Dr. *The Cat in the Hat*. New York: Random House, 1957.

Taylor, Jack. *One Family Under God*. Nashville: Broadman Press, 1974, pp. 96, 97. Quote used by permission.

Time. "Letters Home," Nov. 24, 1975, pp. 101-102.

Timone, George A. *New York Times*, October 30, 1955, p. 73.

Toffler, Alvin. *Future Shock*. New York: Random House, 1970.

Tolkien, J. R. R. *The Hobbit*. Boston: Houghton Mifflin, 1966.

Tournier, Paul. *Adventure of Living*. New York: Harper & Row, 1965.

Tournier, Paul. *The Meaning of Persons*. New York: Harper & Row, 1957.

Tournier, Paul. *The Person Reborn*. New York: Harper & Row, 1966.

Tournier, Paul. *To Understand Each Other*. Richmond, Va.: John Knox Press, 1962.

Treasury of Sermon Illustrations. Nashville: Abingdon Press, 1950, p. 166. Quote from Ernestine Schuman-Heink.